GREAT WHITETAIL HUNTS
And The Lessons They Taught

Great Whitetail Hunts
And The Lessons They Taught

Venture Press

Bigfork, Montana

GREAT WHITETAIL HUNTS And The Lessons They Taught.

Published by David Morris, Venture Press, P.O. Box 1689,
Bigfork, MT 59911 in cooperation with *North American WHITETAIL* magazine, Game & Fish Publications,
2250 Newmarket Pkwy., Suite 110, Marietta, GA 30067.

Printed in the United States of America.
First Edition.

Edited by Ken Dunwoody.

Designed and produced by Tom Bulloch, Bulloch & Associates,
P.O. Box 6247, Woodland Park, CO 80866.

Proofed by Maureen Meyer.

Library of Congress Catalog Card Number: 95-060953

ISBN 0-9633315-2-3

Dedication

To whitetail hunters everywhere
who realize that the journey, not the trophy,
is the greatest reward of hunting.

Table Of Contents

Acknowledgements XI

Foreword by David Morris XII

Introduction by Ken Dunwoody XVI

Chapter 1 - **Illinois' Land Of The Giants** by Stan Potts 18

Chapter 2 - **Monster Of The Muskeg** by Gordon Whittington 34

Chapter 3 - **Wyoming's Last-Ditch Whitetail** by Dick Idol 50

Chapter 4 - **A Buck For The Old Guys** by Bob Haney 64

Chapter 5 - **The Third-Wish Trophy** by Steve Vaughn 80

Chapter 6 - **Magic & Madness In The Montana Mountains** by David Morris 94

Chapter 7 - **Winning On The Road** by Jay Gates 112

Chapter 8 - **Saskatchewan's Wild-Card Buck** by Jim Shockey 124

Chapter 9 - **The Ghost Of Boggy Slough** by Dr. James C. Kroll 136

Chapter 10 - **A Father's Greatest Trophy** by Rick Vaughn 148

Chapter 11 - **Hunting The Invisible Buck** by Greg Miller 158

Chapter 12 - **In Search Of A Texas Trophy** by Bob Zaiglin 172

Chapter 13 - **Beating The Jinx** by Les Davenport 182

Acknowledgements

by Ken Dunwoody

THIS COLLECTION of deer hunting stories never could have been published without the considerable help of others. I am indebted to the 13 hunters whose stories are included in this book, but especially to David Morris and Gordon Whittington, whose additional contributions helped me immeasurably. Thanks are also due to Tom Bulloch for his layout and design, to Rita Head and Maureen Meyer for their proofreading and technical expertise and to Game & Fish Publications, Inc., for the opportunity to handle this project.

I cannot adequately thank my parents, who made sure I learned to hunt, always encouraged my writing career and, in their everyday actions, taught me the value of ethics, responsibility and family. Nor can I truly express my gratitude to my wife, Patricia, whose journalistic talent is exceeded only by her patience and unfailing willingness to help. And to my son, Jonathan, who never complained when my work on this book interfered with our baseball and fishing time, I offer my thanks and apologies. I am busy making amends.

Foreword
by David Morris

THEY ARE BURNED INTO MY MEMORY FOREVER — the high-adventure hunting stories of the old greats, men such as Jack O'Connor, Charlie Elliott, Ben East, Elmer Keith and Nash Buckingham.

As a callow youth growing up in South Alabama, where the biggest "big game" around was an overgrown 'coon or 'possum, I used to eagerly read every big game hunting story I could get my hands on. But from the beginning, my hands-down favorite was the adventure story, the kind of dramatic, first-hand tale that let me imagine I was hunting right alongside the author. I would hang on every word, allowing my fertile imagination to reconstruct the setting in my mind while I lived out every heartbeat and sensation. I felt the cold, the heat, the fear, the dejection, the weariness and the thrill of the hunt as if it were my own.

Hunting was definitely in my blood, but from my perspective in the pineywoods of Alabama, I had no reason to believe I would ever get any closer to big game hunting than the pages of books or magazines. Those stories were my gateway to an exotic world of adventure, wild beast and faraway places.

Then, in my mid-teen years, an unexpected event moved my dreams ever closer to becoming reality. Whitetail deer were stocked near my hometown! While a dozen or so deer scattered across hundreds of square miles may not actually qualify as much of an opportunity, just knowing they were out there somewhere was all the excuse I needed to "hunt deer." And hunt them I did — weekends, holidays, before school, after school and, yes, even during school on the rare occasion that I actually came across a fresh deer track.

In the beginning, I don't think I truly expected to kill a deer. To have real expectations, you have to be able to imagine the event in your mind, and try as I might, I couldn't conjure up an image of me actually seeing and shooting a buck. The scene was just too far-fetched to imagine, though I certainly tried. Still, the book and magazine stories reassured me that such a thing was possible, at least for others in some distant land, such as Texas, Pennsylvania, Maine or Wisconsin.

My prospects took a giant turn for the better, however, when I met a little lady in college who would eventually become my wife. She lived across the state in southwest Alabama near the Tombigbee River, where rumor had it that there were lots of deer in the riverbottom swamps. You can guess the rest.

Through what amounted to begging, I persuaded my girlfriend to arrange a hunt along the Tombigbee with her uncle, Edward Mills. I eventually found myself in a world that was practically unbelievable.

Deer were everywhere — more than I thought existed on the planet! Unfortunately, because I was gawking more than hunting, I came up short on my first attempts. But finally, I managed to fulfill my lifelong dream — kill a whitetail buck!

I can't honestly say that I expected to ever take another buck. I hadn't thought that far ahead. To claim that one deer, to achieve that milestone, seemed accomplishment enough. But by the grace of the Good Lord, what lay beyond that first buck exceeded my wildest dreams!

Through a series of unlikely events, I later became the owner/manager of one of the largest deer hunting plantations in the South and partner/editor of Game & Fish Publications, a company that ultimately grew to publish hunting and fishing magazines nationwide, including *North American WHITETAIL*. From that point on, my hunting fantasies came true one by one. First, there were whitetails by the score, then trips to Canada, Alaska, the West, Europe and, ultimately, Africa. Every step of the way, I lived out the dreams that had begun long ago with my "friends," Jack O'Connor, Charlie Elliott, Ben East and the others.

Somewhere along the way, I discovered that I had started with the best — the whitetail deer. No matter where or what I hunted, I kept coming back to whitetails because no other game offers the challenge of a trophy buck. With other animals, I was content to hunt them successfully once or twice. Not so with the whitetail!

So now, I've come full circle, back to the animal that started it all. But, the one thing that hasn't changed is my love for a good hunting tale. These days, I seem to seek out trophy whitetail stories more than anything else. Each one rekindles the excitement, mystery and high adventure that held me spellbound so many years ago. That's what this book, **GREAT WHITETAIL HUNTS And The Lessons They Taught,** is all about — shared excitement, mystery and adventure for all who long for autumn, the thrill of the chase and the sight of a big-racked buck. And who knows, somewhere in the backwoods or perhaps even in a crowded city subdivision, a kid just might find his dreams born within these pages.

GREAT WHITETAIL HUNTS
And The Lessons They Taught

Introduction

by Ken Dunwoody

WE'VE ALL BEEN THERE.

If you've hunted whitetails long enough and hard enough, you have probably enjoyed some success. Certainly, you've endured some failures. And if you're a serious hunter, you've learned plenty of lessons along the way, too.

The 13 hunters we've featured in this book are no exception. They've all taken big whitetails — some of them world-class trophies — during their hunting careers. But, they also have suffered through the same sorts of frustrations and blunders we all have. In fact, I think you'll find these hunters have encountered some nightmares you've never even imagined, and each of their hunts are haunted by moments of anxiety, self-loathing and downright despair. But, each hunt also offered a unique challenge and, in one way or another, ultimately ended in triumph.

Some of the events they describe will sound all-too-familiar; others will be startlingly unique. What do you do, for example, when a huge buck won't emerge from behind a propane tank? What if the biggest eight-pointer in history is standing a few feet underneath you and you can't draw your bow? How do you rebound after missing chances at two Boone and Crockett bucks in a half-hour's time? What's it like to follow the same buck for five years? And, what tricks do you pull out of your hat in the final hours of a do-or-die hunt?

From Canada to Texas to Wisconsin to South Carolina, we've

brought together a remarkable collection of true deer hunting stories from a remarkable group of hunters. Each man shares the story of his most memorable trophy hunts, and allows us to go along for the ride. It's a rare insight into the minds and strategies of some dedicated deer hunters, and a revealing look at how each man coped with some of the biggest moments of his hunting career.

Besides pure excitement (and at times, comic relief), these stories also provide a special bonus. We've asked each hunter to share his own personal tips, tactics and secrets learned or applied on these hunts, and we've highlighted those within each story. Together, they provide some of the accumulated wisdom of 13 veteran outdoorsmen who have combined for a couple of centuries of deer hunting experience.

But more than anything else, these stories are fun to read. If you've never huddled in a treestand in sub-zero cold or still-hunted at midday in 90-degree temperatures, you can now experience it from the comfort of your easy chair. Along the way, you'll try to outwit a huge buck in the Alberta muskeg, search for wide-racked trophies in the mesquite of South Texas, hunt the most amazing 10-acre tract you could ever imagine and relive an unbelievably wild hunt in the mountains of Montana.

That's what this book is all about — capturing the nerve-rattling thrills, the hope, the anxiety, the strategies and the exhilaration of pursuing giant whitetails. It's the essence of deer hunting, all wrapped up in 13 unforgettable hunts. It's been a privilege to work with these hunters and to bring their stories together in this book. I hope you feel the same way about reading it.

CHAPTER ONE

Illinois' Land Of The Giants

by Stan Potts

HOW MANY TIMES CAN A MAN GET THE CHANCE OF A LIFETIME?

For three amazing years in the early 1980s, my friends and I hunted in a place where once-in-a lifetime events seemed to happen over and over again. It was our own "Field of Dreams," except that it was in Illinois, not Iowa. And, it was populated not with legendary ballplayers, but with legendary whitetails. It may not have been heaven, but as I look back now, it sure came close.

For us, nirvana was a 10-acre tract in the middle of the Prairie State, located near Clinton Lake in DeWitt County. The property we had permission to hunt was situated next to some state-operated conservation land that hadn't been hunted in many years. With the lake and adjacent waterways along with woodlots, corn fields and bean fields, it was a remarkable place in a state that's famous for remarkable deer.

While we knew we had a great spot, we didn't truly appreciate just how special this place was until an amazing string of encounters eventually led to a showdown with the second-greatest whitetail in the history of Illinois bowhunting. Best of all, we had it all to ourselves. Still, like a rookie ballplayer suddenly thrust into the big leagues, I had a lot to learn in those days. And from my very first season on the property, the big bucks did their best to educate me.

My first teacher was Wally. That was just his nickname, of course.

In three seasons of hunting a remarkable 10-acre tract in central Illinois, the author and his partners had several encounters with world-class bucks. But, none were better than this monstrous whitetail, which scored 195 5/8 Boone and Crockett points and is the No. 2 all-time typical bowkill in the state. Photo by Brenda Potts.

By utilizing rattling antlers — along with the lessons learned from earlier failures — the author coaxed this giant 11-pointer straight into the record book. The B&C trophy features tines as long as 13 inches and an inside spread of 23 2/8 inches. Photo by Mike Chapman.

His full name, at least to us, was "Wallhanger," and he was the largest-bodied, biggest-racked buck we'd ever seen.

Doug Tilley, one of my hunting partners, was the first to get a glimpse of Wally. His excited description of the big deer was all the motivation I needed to head into the woods with John Piatt, my other hunting partner, on October 21, 1981. It was one of the first times we had hunted the property, and it also was opening day of the waterfowl season in Illinois. I had grilled Doug with questions about the buck until I was sure I could recognize Wally on sight. Now, we just had to find him.

Sitting in a treestand that morning, I could hear the occasional sounds of duck calls and shotgun blasts coming from the coves of Clinton

Lake just a few hundred yards away. No other upland game or deer hunters were allowed in the Clinton area, so things were pretty quiet otherwise. There was still a lot of foliage on the trees, but everything was blanketed in a coat of frost. Because of the cold, I was wearing a stocking face-mask, the kind with two openings for your eyes but none for your nose or mouth.

Suddenly, I spotted antler tines emerging over a rise about 30 yards away. The buck was moving slowly, but through a small opening in the thicket, I could see that he was drifting toward me. He was looking bigger with every step.

Never before had I seen such a giant whitetail. His dark rack was enormous, with six tines on the left and five on the right. Surely this was "Wally," the 190-inch-class buck Doug had described. The regal-looking deer stopped behind a red haw bush on the ridge and stood perfectly motionless. I held my breath and waited for his next move. When it came, it wasn't what I expected. Instead of continuing his slow, casual pace, Wally suddenly broke into a trot! But he was coming straight toward my tree, on a course that would bring him right under my stand.

Almost instinctively, I came to full draw. He was approaching faster now, getting closer and closer. When he came into bow range, I decided to whistle, figuring he would stop when he heard the unexpected sound. But, I'd forgotten about the face mask. Again and again, I tried to muster an audible whistle, but the mask muffled every attempt. Frantically, I followed him with my arrow, trying to make some noise that would cause the buck to stop. He kept coming.

> ***When a moving deer reaches the spot where I want to shoot him, I make a soft grunting noise to stop him long enough to get a good shot. But, be sure that you're already at full draw before you grunt just in case the buck looks in your direction when he hears the sound.***

Almost in shock, I watched as Wally passed my stand broadside at just 12 yards, still on the run. Swinging the bow with him, I made my play and touched the release. The arrow ripped through the cold air — and buried itself in the ground 10 feet behind the disappearing deer. That buck never even knew he'd been shot at! Jumping a fence, he disappeared into the corn field.

That was my first experience with a world-class buck. By all rights, it should have been my last, because encounters with such behemoths are exceptionally rare, even for skilled hunters in the best of habitat. I didn't yet have the experience I needed to make the right decisions and overcome the rattled nerves that accompany the sighting of a monster buck. But, it wasn't my last chance. In fact, my education had only begun, and fate had determined that I would learn my lessons the hard way.

Four days later, John and I were in our evening stands, which were closer to the picked corn field than our previous locations. My stand was on the fenceline along the property's south side, while John's was about 75 yards away next to the west fence. Shelled corn littered the ground of the adjacent 10-acre field, which provided an attractive food source for deer wandering among the cut corn stalks.

Directly west of John was a ditch and a small patch of timber that separated our 10 acres from a large soybean field on the state-run conservation land. That evening, while we were on our stands, a farmer began combining the bean field.

It wasn't long before a majestic buck stepped boldly out of the brush. He stood motionless for awhile, watching the corn field, before jumping the fence. Unfortunately, he was still 50 or 60 yards from John, which was too far for a comfortable bow shot.

As I watched that whitetail, I saw another buck jump the same fence crossing. Then another one followed ... and another. Finally, a fifth buck crossed the fence and began feeding with the other four. Evidently, the farmer's combining had caused all the bucks to skirt the edge of the field and cross the fence at that same point.

All five were dandies. I figured the smallest would score about 135, but the biggest was a dark-horned, 10-point bruiser with 170 to 175 inches of antlers. The group milled around in the field, always staying about 100 yards away from our stands.

Suddenly, a doe appeared at the same crossing, hopped the fence and began feeding on the corn. It was still several days before rutting activity would begin, and sometimes at that stage of the season, bucks just don't like to have does feeding in the same area. The dark-horned buck looked up and stared at the intruder. I could tell from his posture that he didn't want that doe around. He lowered his head, stretched his neck out and started trotting toward her. She saw him coming and immediately high-tailed it out of the field, jumping the fence right under John's tree stand. The buck chased her for a moment, but he pulled up and stopped about 50 yards from John.

It was from a tree stand near this spot that the author rattled up and arrowed his trophy whitetail. His hunting property, which was adjacent to unhunted parcels operated by the state and Illinois Power Company, was brimming with big bucks. Photo by Gordon Whittington.

After watching the doe for a minute, the buck looked from side to side and slowly ambled back into the corn field. He actually seemed to be proud of himself for running off the doe. But 30 seconds later, she was back, feeding in the corn. Once again the buck chased her out of the field. She jumped the fence under John's stand, but the buck again stopped his pursuit just beyond bow range. This happened three more times as poor John watched helplessly. Each of us grunted several times, but neither had any luck coaxing a buck within range.

We sat and watched those five big bucks for the rest of the evening. They were still there when darkness came and we finally climbed down from our stands to go home. It had been a frustrating outing and, as it turned out, a frustrating season.

Undaunted, we returned in 1982. On November 4, with the rut approaching, Doug and I headed back to the 10 acres for an afternoon of hunting. John planned to join us after work at 4 p.m., which would give him about 90 minutes of hunting time. At 55 degrees with a light south-

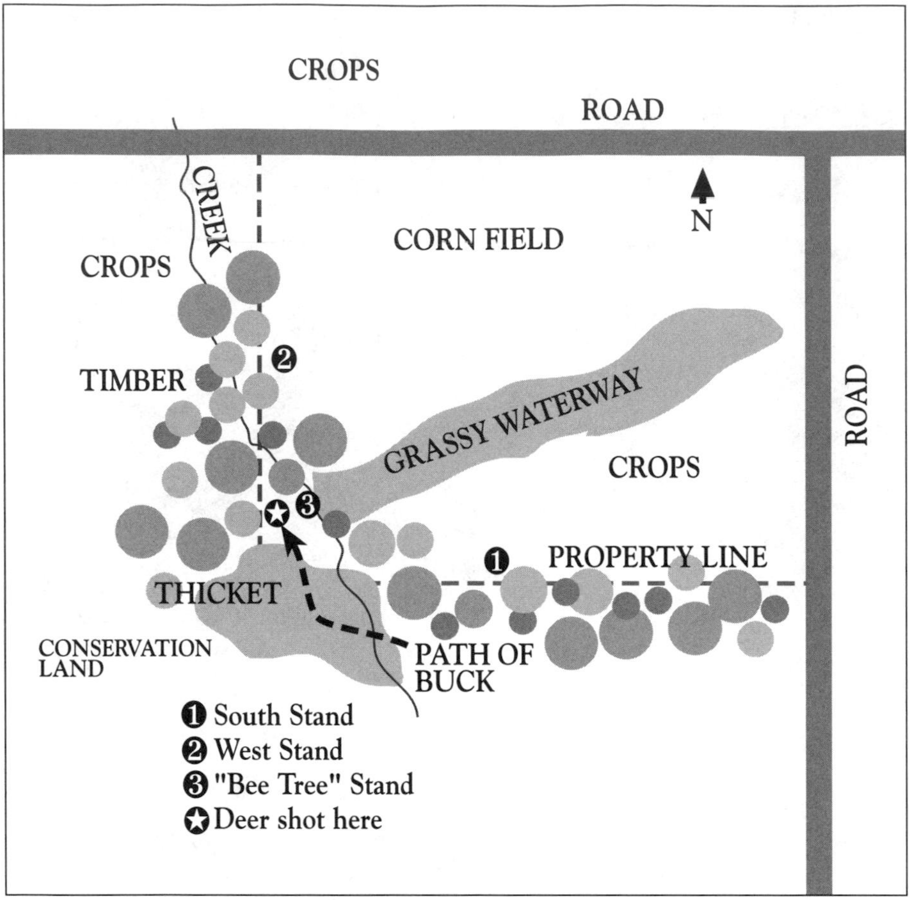

With exclusive permission to hunt this prime 10-acre tract, the author and his partners were able to see several record-class whitetails. After frustrating encounters at the south stand in 1981 and the west stand in 1982, he later claimed Illinois' second-biggest typical bowkill ever from "the bee tree."

west wind and clear skies, it was a pleasant day.

Everything had been very quiet until, quite suddenly, I heard a loud commotion in the thicket behind my tree stand. There was no mistaking the sound of a buck tearing up a tree! Out of the corner of my eye, I saw a big whitetail raking his antlers up and down the length of a tree, snapping off branches with every pass. I stood up as gradually as I could, trying to hide behind the trunk of the tree to disguise my movements. After taking my bow off the hook, I slowly turned around to get a good look at the deer.

He was 50 yards from my stand, rubbing his rack on a willow tree that had a trunk about the size of my leg. A giant buck with a snow-white rack, he would be known to us as Whitey. I didn't think I'd ever see another deer that could compare to Wally, but this one — while not quite as heavy — was equally awesome. Whitey had some of the longest tines I'd ever seen on a deer in my life.

As I watched from my stand, Whitey tore that willow tree apart. I knew that when he finished, there were three directions he might head. He could walk down the run, which would bring him directly underneath my stand; he might follow a little waterway that led up to a pond about 150 yards to the south; or he could travel down the waterway, directly toward Doug.

Whitey finally finished mauling the tree and hopped the ditch, coming straight toward me. His head was down as he lumbered slowly along the trail, exhibiting that characteristic gait that makes huge bucks look as though they are going to fall over with every step. I could feel my heart pounding as I watched him come up a slight rise, head still low, striding directly toward my stand. But just as he topped the hill, Whitey raised his head and stared right at me. Even though I was behind the tree trunk, I realized that I was silhouetted against the sky in back of me. Whitey couldn't quite make out what I was, but he knew something didn't look right.

When hunting on the edge of a thicket that borders an open field, careful stand placement is necessary to avoid being backlit, or silhouetted, from the perspective of the deer. You should position your stand 15 to 20 yards away from the place where you expect the deer to emerge. You don't want him to walk straight at your stand, or he'll be looking right at you. Instead, try to create a situation where he'll walk past your location on one side or the other.

Immediately, he began moving his head back and forth, his huge rack swaying, as he became more nervous by the second. While I watched, frozen in place, he stomped his foot, took four or five steps backward, and then turned and walked the other way. He was headed away from me, but straight toward Doug.

Whitey jumped across the ditch and began to work a scrape, raising up on his hind legs and rubbing his antlers and head in the limbs of a burly white oak. Suddenly, I heard a noise from out in the field. It was John, who had apparently just arrived and was headed down the fenceline toward his stand! Fortunately, he saw my desperate hand signals and squatted in the weeds next to the fence. He realized I must be watching a buck.

Apprehensively, I turned my attention back to Whitey. He was looking in John's direction, but he soon lost interest and returned to the scrape. After a few minutes, he resumed his route toward Doug.

I knew Doug would get a shot at him. I waited and watched, expecting something to happen any second. I was even leaning out of the tree, trying to get a better view of the deer. Seconds later, I heard the sound of a bow shot. I could see the buck take three or four big leaps forward then stop. Whitey looked all around, as if trying to figure out what had just happened. Moments later, he began walking away, disappearing over the hill.

I knew Doug had to have been within 15 yards of the deer when he shot, so the arrow must have traveled completely through the buck. Sometimes when that happens, I knew a mortally wounded deer will just flinch and walk away, not knowing that it's been hit. We'd find the deer nearby, I figured.

By now, John had continued on to his stand, but there was no sign of Doug. I decided he must be waiting before pursuing the deer. After an hour or so, John climbed down from his tree and walked over to mine, anxious to know what had happened. When I saw Doug coming our way, I knew we'd get the full story.

The best time to select stand locations is when you're doing your post-season scouting during the months of January, February and March. All of the sign from the previous season's rutting activity is still visible at this time, and you can use trails, rubs, scrapes, feeding and bedding areas to determine your best stand choices. This is also the best time to clear shooting lanes, so that you don't disturb the area too close to hunting season. Remember, mature bucks have an uncanny ability to stay behind the only branch you didn't trim, so be sure to cut away all the vegetation that could get in your way.

We did, unfortunately. With his head down, Doug trudged up to us and explained how he had missed Whitey. Instead of grunting and stopping the buck in a clear shooting lane, Doug tried a shot that wound up deflecting off a limb. The arrow had sailed harmlessly over the giant buck's back. It was just another example of what could go wrong if you didn't cover all the bases. We'd learned another lesson, compliments of Whitey. But had we blown our best chances?

A few days later, I was in that same stand near the edge of the corn field. With the rut in gear, I had decided to bring my rattling antlers this time.

Several deer passed by, but none I wanted to shoot — especially since I knew what kind of monsters were wandering around that area. Then, as I was scanning the terrain in front of me, I spotted a big deer emerging from the timber on the far side of the corn field. Quickly finding him in my binoculars, I could tell he was a great buck. If only I could get him within range.

When the buck passed behind a rise in the corn field, I took advantage of the opportunity and began rattling my antlers. Because the deer was 400 yards away, I performed a loud, fierce rattling sequence to make sure he could hear it. The deer was already headed in my general direction, so I hoped the rattling would bring him directly to me. As soon as I finished, I quickly hung the antlers on a limb and grabbed my bow.

All of a sudden, I heard another deer behind me, just over my right shoulder. It was coming in fast, walking noisily through the dry leaves, apparently looking for the source of the antler rattling. I raised my bow up over a little limb and turned completely around on my stand.

The area behind me was a thicket, full of red haw, honey locust and multiflora rose. I still couldn't see the deer, but I could hear the leaves crunching with his every step. The sounds grew louder and louder, until it seemed that the deer must be right beneath my tree. Suddenly, it stepped out from behind a multiflora rose bush to my right. With head down and hair bristling, he looked ready for a fight.

The buck's big main beams had tines stacked on them like a picket fence! He was a giant, and he was headed for an opening right behind my stand. That would put him broadside from me at about 12 yards. Ever so slowly, I raised my bow and began putting tension on the string to begin my draw. But without warning, about two steps before he reached the opening, the buck did a little stutter-step and began walking away from me. That cagey old whitetail must have had a sixth sense that just wouldn't let him step into the opening. Before I knew it, he had melted away into the thicket.

My heart was pounding. What could I do? With my lack of experience, I was convinced the buck was getting away and that I needed to try something to turn him around. I reached over to my rattling antlers still hanging in the tree, grabbed them with one hand and gave them a shake. What I didn't realize was that the buck was still nearby, hidden by the brush. He apparently saw my frantic move and spooked instantly. He looked as big as a cow as he bolted out of the brush, leaped across the ditch and galloped out of sight. As I watched the buck make his getaway, I just about got sick. What a stupid mistake! Dejectedly, I turned around in the stand and slumped into my seat, heartsick over another missed opportunity.

Movement is a major reason hunters are detected by deer, whether those hunters are on the ground or in a treestand. For that reason, always keep your bow and rattling antlers secure, quiet and close at hand. You should be able to reach them and prepare for a shot with as little movement as possible.

All of a sudden, I saw a patch of brown in front of my stand. I had completely forgotten about the first buck, the one I had originally been rattling for! He was now only 60 yards away, with his head down, following a waterway that would lead him right by my tree. As I squared around to prepare for the shot, I accidentally bumped the rattling antlers. They slipped off the limb, crashed against the platform of my stand and, before I could catch them, tumbled out of the tree and fell onto the wire fence below me. There, suspended on a wire strand by the rope that held them together, the antlers swung back and forth, clanking against each other repeatedly.

You know the rest of the story. It took that buck about two seconds to disappear from sight. I found myself wishing for the rope that held those two rattling antlers together. If I had it, I'd have used that rope to hang myself from the tree! Two monster bucks had been right in front of me, and I had messed up my chances for both of them. How stupid could I get?

I already had seen more huge deer than most hunters do in a lifetime, and I had nothing to show for it. We had learned a few valuable lessons, to be sure, but I found myself wishing we could have learned them while hunting some smaller deer. Though costly, the experience I'd gained might yet prove valuable. If I could somehow get one more chance ...

That opportunity, as it turned out, didn't present itself until the next season, in 1983, on an unseasonably warm afternoon. Even though it was November 21, the temperature had climbed to 70 degrees by the time I made it to my stand at 2:30 p.m. When I arrived there, I discovered a rather unique problem. Dozens of honey bees were swarming around the bur oak, just below my portable stand. Normally, Illinois' frigid November weather would have rendered the bees inactive, so this was a highly unlikely scenario. I considered trying another stand location and even took a few steps back toward the truck. But something — call it intuition or just a feeling — made me hesitate. For some reason, I felt I had to get into that tree stand. I'd come up empty during the recent three day shotgun hunt, and I was now determined to get my buck with a bow.

My climb through the swirling bees was long, slow and anxious, but fortunately, I made it into the stand without incident. The bees kept their swarm below the platform and were soon forgotten. I had bigger things on my mind.

No matter how carefully or quietly you try to approach your stand or hunting location, the surrounding area is always disturbed by your arrival. Before you begin rattling, grunting or using calls, you should wait several minutes to let everything settle down and return to its normal, natural state.

I settled in with my bow and rattling horns. Even though the peak of the rut had begun to taper off, this was still a period of major deer movement. Most of the does had been bred already, so the bucks were really having to travel to search out those last few does in estrus. This would create an ideal scenario for rattling.

My approach had frightened off the birds and squirrels, so I decided to wait for 15 minutes and let the area settle down. Because the southwest winds were very light, I knew the sound of clashing antlers would travel quite a distance. I started my first rattling sequence hard and loud, keeping it going for about 90 seconds. When I finished, I carefully hung up the antlers and grabbed my bow. A 10-minute wait produced no sign of a buck, so I tried again. This second sequence was much softer, with a few grunt calls mixed in. The idea was to entice any reluctant buck that may have hesitated on his approach. But none appeared.

Before long, I decided to sit down for awhile. As I did, I was careful to hang my bow very close to me so that very little movement would be necessary to retrieve it. Within 20 minutes, a doe appeared in the corner of a bean field about 50 yards away. Behind her was a 140-class, 3 1/2-year-old buck, soon followed by a smaller 120-class buck. The lead buck chased the doe relentlessly, but she wanted no part of him. Within minutes she disappeared in the direction from which she had come, with both her suitors in hot pursuit. I kept looking, hoping for something bigger.

An hour after my first rattling attempt, I decided to run through another sequence. I did a minute of hard rattling, then stood up in my stand, bow in hand, and waited. I was watching an open corn field to the northeast, about 50 yards away, when my attention was diverted by the sound of a twig snapping. Slowly, I looked to my left, only to discover a squirrel. I shifted my attention back to the corn field.

But, there was more noise coming from the squirrel's direction, and this time it sounded different. I turned again — and caught my breath. It was a deer, a gigantic buck, 50 yards south of my stand and looking for a fight. To my amazement, he was the biggest-framed typical buck I'd ever seen — even more impressive than Wally and Whitey. My partners and I had seen several trophies in the last two years that would qualify for the Boone and Crockett record book but nothing like this brute.

Those first couple seasons of hunting this acreage had provided us with a wealth of experience in dealing with mature whitetails. Now, it was time to find out if that experience was going to pay off.

Turning his massive head from side to side, the buck investigated the area as he skirted the edge of a thicket opposite my stand. A quick look at his path indicated that he would come out on the other side of the thicket, where there were two runs. One would put him 20 yards from my stand, the other 40 yards out. Both trails went right past my tree, with shooting lanes already cleared for each one.

I gently turned to position myself for a shot as I watched for the buck to reappear from the thicket. When he finally did, he was coming down the 20-yard run! If he kept coming, he'd pass behind a red haw bush, giving me a chance to bring my bow to full draw. But as he was passing behind the bush, he stopped, nose to the ground, with only his head and antlers exposed.

I held at full draw as we both stood motionless in the still woods. Finally, he started walking again, edging closer to my stand. When the deer cleared the bush, he was quartering away from me and going downhill. I had to put my 20-yard pin higher and farther behind his shoulder to reach the vitals.

It was now or never. I touched the button on my thumb release and saw the arrow bury itself to the fletching. Instantly, the buck spun around and, in three leaps, was out of sight. I could hear him crashing through the brush for 10 or 15 seconds Then, it was deathly quiet.

Although I knew it was a good hit, it seemed unnatural for the arrow to be so high and far back. Because it had all happened so quickly, I started to second-guess myself. That's when my belated case of buck fever struck. I was a nervous wreck. Trying to stay composed, I told myself to wait 30 minutes before getting down from the tree. But, it was impossible to wait. An agonizingly slow 10 minutes dragged by before my nerves gave out. I climbed down and went to town for help. When I showed up at the back door of John's house, he could tell immediately by the look on my face that something had happened.

I told him I needed help because I had just shot one of the biggest bucks I'd ever seen — quite a statement considering all those giants we'd been hunting the last two years. When I explained to John that I thought I had shot a 10-pointer, he seemed disappointed. "Just a 10, huh?" he asked. After all, we had rattled in a 180-class 6x6 just last week and had seen several other B&C-class bucks. I told John that the deer wasn't "just a 10" but was, instead, the biggest-framed whitetail I'd seen.

We decided that we might need some more help, so we went to get Kirby North. He'd heard our stories of monster bucks on the 10 acres and had made me promise to call him if I ever shot one. Kirby questioned me at length as we gathered our tracking lights and headed back to the lease, but it's hard to describe a gross 200-inch typical to someone who has never seen one. All my descriptions did little to prepare him for what we were about to find.

Whenever you can, try to wait until a whitetail goes behind a tree or bush before you draw back your bow. If the buck is standing still, don't draw until he turns his head away from you. The temptation to come to full draw can be enormous, but you must wait until the deer gives you an opportunity. If he sees you moving, you won't get another chance.

When we reached my stand, we had no trouble finding the initial blood trail. It was easy to follow for the first 50 or 60 yards. Then, there was no blood trail at all. The last drop was about three feet up on a

The author's huge 1983 trophy (being held at lower left) was the biggest buck he'd ever taken, but it wasn't the only one. These other two whitetails already graced the walls of his Illinois home. Photo by Jack Ehresman.

sapling, so we started making small circles from there, trying to find another speck of blood. The buck had apparently gone into a field of tall switch grass, which made the tracking job even more difficult. We marked the last spot with a handkerchief.

John and Kirby followed a fenceline to see if the buck had jumped across anywhere. Meanwhile, I decided to follow a downward slope that led back in the direction from which the buck had first come. I figured a mortally wounded animal would most likely use the downhill route to circle back, so I began to cast my light back and forth on the hill. When I noticed a big scrape by a tree to my left, I instinctively shined my light toward it. When I did, I saw the big right side of his antlers sticking up over the grass.

I ran to the buck, almost unable to believe my eyes. I knew he was a giant, but I still wasn't ready for the reality of his massive antlers. I sat down and put his head in my lap to count the points. For a few moments, I was flooded with emotion, in part because of the sadness that such a great animal was dead. Yet, I was also elated because I had finally accomplished what I'd set out to do.

After my private moment with the buck, I stood up to look for John and Kirby. They were about 100 yards away when I yelled that I had found the buck. All I could see were their flashlights bobbing around as they ran through the grass and trees to meet me. When they arrived, I shined my light on the buck. At first they were in shock, but it wasn't long before we all began to jump up and down, high-fiving in celebration. Kirby kept saying, "Your quest is over ... your quest is over ... nobody is going to believe this!"

We field-dressed the buck and dragged him to the truck. Three-fourths of the arrow had been inside the body cavity, we discovered, but there was no exit wound. That explained why there hadn't been much of a blood trail. We drove the deer to the archery shop in town about 8 p.m., where phone calls to our friends created a crowd that kept us up until midnight.

Remarkably enough, when the official measuring was completed, the buck wound up as the No. 2 typical whitetail ever killed with a bow in Illinois. His net score was a staggering 195 5/8, complete with a 23 2/8-inch inside spread. As it turned out, he had 11 points, including 13-inch G-2s.

It had taken two years — and some heart-breaking misses — to set the stage for that last encounter. But thanks to the hard-earned lessons of those early failures, I finally was ready when opportunity knocked ... yet again.

CHAPTER TWO

Monster Of The Muskeg

by Gordon Whittington

WHAT ILLNESS DO YOU MOST DREAD COMING DOWN WITH IN DEER SEASON?

Some might suggest the flu, others a nasty sinus infection or even the common cold. Any of those could keep you at home when you'd much rather be in the woods. But, my own vote would go to a malady that's undeniably devastating, yet at the same time so subtle a hunter seldom even realizes he has it until the damage has been done. Forget rabies, tetanus and Lyme disease, folks — I'm talking about good old brain cramps.

Ah, those maddening little lapses of rational thought that so often end up costing us dearly — make that deerly — during whitetail season. The fact that so many hunters suffer from their effects is the single greatest reason many bucks die of old age in this era of heavy hunting pressure.

There was a time when I believed brain cramps were solely the domain of beginning deer hunters. I made every possible sort of strategic error in my early years of chasing whitetails, and I really expected to grow out of that. One day, I figured, I'd be able to use my head for something other than just a place to hang a camouflage cap. So, I plodded along, secure in the knowledge that after I had a few more years of hunting expe-

The author's big 4x4 Alberta whitetail, which featured impressive width and tine length, grossed 154 Boone & Crockett points. It was actually the smaller of two trophy bucks that had been sighted in the area! Photo by Byron Stewart.

rience, I'd really understand big bucks and would be able to bag every one I pursued.

It pains me to report that I was wrong. Today, nearly 35 years after my first whitetail hunt, I realize that brain cramps are not just a childhood disease. For proof, I submit to you the story of my 1994 hunt in Alberta, Canada.

Imagine, if you will, traveling to a part of the world renowned for the size of its deer and learning that your host has found for you two trophy bucks in one small area. And get this: He doubts anyone else even will bother to hunt deer in that spot all season.

"Wow!" you're probably saying to yourself right about now. "What I'd give to be able to go to one of the world's best places for big whitetails and stake out a hotspot like that! Imagine knowing exactly where two monster bucks are and being able to park yourself right in that area day

Margarita and Marvin Pischke got everyone in camp fired up when they brought in these two handsome whitetails on November 12. Both deer were taken in a farmland hunting zone and were heavily into the rut, a buck's most vulnerable time. Photo by Gordon Whittington.

after day — during the rut, no less!"

Yes, that might indeed be what you're saying to yourself, and if so, I don't blame you. But, my own response to such news was, well, a bit less enthusiastic. Oh, I had my reasons, which at the time seemed valid enough. But in retrospect, I can only be thankful that this particular spell of brain cramps lasted just six days, instead of all 8 1/2 I had set aside to hunt.

Byron Stewart, who operates Tracks 'n Trails Outfitting in the small town of Cynthia, told my longtime hunting buddy Tommy Witt and me about these two bucks upon our arrival on Thursday, November 10. Tommy, an experienced hunter of Canadian whitetails, agreed with me that the situation had potential; however, it wasn't something he could take advantage of. His whitetail permit was for a farmland hunting unit several miles east of where these bucks had been seen. Fellow hunters Steve Ninemire and Travis Pate, who'd be joining us over the weekend, would be hunting the same unit as Tommy. But, I'd booked this hunt too late to get one of those coveted farmland permits, but I was glad to get any whitetail permit on short notice. Now, my tardiness, it seemed, could turn out to be an advantage, for I was the only guy in camp who could legally go after the two bucks Byron had found.

But, there were questions to be answered first. For starters, in what sort of place had they been seen? Just as critical to my assessment of the situation, what were the chances that either deer was still there?

The area where the sightings had occurred, we soon learned, is more a moose swamp than deer woods. Traditionally, whitetail hunting in Alberta takes place primarily in agricultural settings, such as the grain fields and scattered woodlots the other guys in camp would be hunting. But, there is no farming within several miles of where these bucks had been spotted. The only "fields" in the vicinity yield oil and natural gas, not grain. This portion of west-central Alberta is a rolling, timbered transition zone between tilled prairies to the east and the rugged Rocky Mountains to the west, and there are incredible petroleum deposits here. (By the way, a well from which Canada Dry gets water for its beverage products also lies in the middle of these oilfields.)

The landscape is, for the most part, what's commonly called "big bush" and is comprised of mile after mile of spruce, aspen (locally known as "poplar"), fir, pine and larch. About the only openings in these vast woods are roads and pipeline right-of-ways (referred to as "cutlines") that allow for the finding, pumping and transporting of crude oil and natural gas. There are few towns of any size in this area; in fact, deer, moose, elk, bears, wolves and other wildlife far outnumber the human inhabitants.

How does an outfitter run across two trophy bucks in a setting so far off the beaten whitetail path? Well, Byron isn't just an outfitter — his primary vocation involves keeping tabs on a number of oil wells for a major petroleum company. That summer, while working an oilfield in this particular swamp, he glimpsed a pair of big bucks standing near one of those groaning oil pumps. The deer's racks were still in velvet and the look was brief, but there was no doubt these were a couple of "shooters." That impression was reinforced a few weeks later when Byron once again saw the bucks, now minus their velvet, in another oilfield openings only a few hundred yards from the scene of the previous encounter.

How good were the two deer? "The smaller one has a really tall rack and should score at least 150 Boone & Crockett," Byron told us. "The other one doesn't have quite as much tine length, but he's a really wide 5x5 with incredible mass. The high-racked buck is a great trophy, but the other one could eat him."

Good news. But, it wasn't clear if the bucks were as huntable as back-to-back sightings might have implied. These woods stretch for miles in every direction and aren't nearly as inviting, from a deer hunter's perspective, as the more open farmland habitat to the east. Alberta residents can hunt whitetails in any unit they wish, and Byron said it was doubtful that any local would bother to hunt that deep in this intimidating cover. Not only are the woods vast, but the ground is covered in many places with a deep layer of sphagnum moss, spruce needles and twigs, the sort of stuff from which peat eventually forms. This "muskeg," as it's called, makes for hard walking and provides little forage for whitetails. Sure enough, there didn't appear to be many deer here, for during scouting trips in the area, Byron hadn't seen even a single doe.

That last fact concerned me most of all. The rut was ready to bust wide open, and I knew these mature bucks wouldn't be missing out on the fun. If there weren't any does where they lived, wouldn't they have simply boarded up their summer homes and headed elsewhere to find some action by now? That argument made sense to me. So, with real doubts that the two deer were still anywhere near where Byron had seen them, I promptly turned my attention elsewhere. Hey, those weren't the only big bucks around.

The lower the deer population and the more balanced the buck:doe ratio, the more likely it is that bucks will roam widely in search of does during the rut. We've all heard that a whitetail lives its entire life in a square-mile area, but that's hardly true, particularly in regard to mature bucks. During the so-called "peak of the rut," you'll usually find a big buck spending his time around doe areas, even if those locations are a mile or more from where he hangs out during the rest of the year.

Six days later, though, I was starting to wonder. We'd spent every minute of legal shooting light still-hunting, rattling and stand-hunting in a huge area of wooded river bottom, clearcuts and "community pasture" many miles from the swamp. Despite it all, I hadn't been able to put myself in the right place at the right time.

The area we'd hunted was a good one. It contained ample sign, and Byron and his clients had shot many big deer there in previous years. On top of that, the rut definitely was heating up. On Saturday, November 12, guide Marvin Pischke had taken advantage of his last free day before the arrival of our other hunters to shoot a big 5x5 in the farm country. What's more, Marvin's wife, Margarita, had taken a solid buck that day as well. Both deer definitely were in rut. While those kills and other scattered sightings of big bucks by our guys in the farm zone were encouraging, by noon on Thursday, November 17, nobody in our party had shot a whitetail. I hadn't yet seen a mature buck that didn't already have one of the Pischkes' tags on it. Something had to give.

Western Alberta is still plenty wild. The author heard the howls of wolves on several occasions and even found their fresh tracks. This wolf, taken by Byron Stewart, was part of a pack that had been killing livestock near the author's hunting site in Alberta. At 80-plus pounds, it's considered small in a region where the big predators often reach 160 pounds. Photo by Gordon Whittington.

Byron and I met Tommy and his guide for a roadside lunch that day. As we warmed up in the truck, we discussed what was proving to be a more-than-challenging hunt. Only 2 1/2 days of hunting remained, and I'm sure Byron could sense my frustration. "Where do you want to go this afternoon?" he asked.

"I don't know," I admitted. "I wonder if we need to look at some new country. Maybe we should try that swamp where you saw those two bucks."

Amazing — it actually had taken me less than a week of not seeing any big bucks to decide I should try hunting where some had been seen. Just goes to show that brain cramps aren't permanent.

We drove north and before long turned into the swampy oilfield, with Byron narrating an overview of the country as we went. Abruptly, the guided tour ended at the exact moment we saw the doe.

She was feeding right out in a clearing, no more than 100 yards off the primary road, at 1 p.m. on a sunny day. What she was doing, however, didn't seem nearly as important right then as the mere fact that she was there. At least one doe lived in this swamp after all. If there were indeed does here, then all of a sudden the chances of finding one of those big bucks hanging around looked a lot better.

Not wanting to alarm the doe, Byron drove on past her to a stopping point perhaps 150 yards farther down the road. Then, we sneaked back to the clearing. Unfortunately, by the time we got there, the doe apparently had fed into the timber because she was nowhere to be found. We decided this was a good place to spend the rest of the afternoon. Looking around, I soon found a hiding spot from which I could watch the opening. Byron returned to the truck with plans to pick me up here at dark.

Not long after settling into my brushpile hideout, which gave me a commanding view of several cutlines and roadcuts, I spotted another doe. She was walking in the opposite direction of the first and was perhaps 400 yards from me. I eyed her through the 9X magnification of my Swarovski scope, hoping to see an antlered companion, but she too was alone.

The fact that shooting light ended without me seeing more deer really didn't disappoint me. I was just thrilled to see that does were in the area. Our most recent snow was now two days old, and it showed that plenty of deer movement had taken place here in that time. There were small tracks, medium-sized tracks and, yes, big tracks. As I discussed these findings with Byron that evening, I learned that I'd been sitting near where he'd spotted the two big bucks earlier in the fall.

Dawn on Friday found me huddled in that same brushpile. The moon had been full overnight, and while I figured that would cause another flurry of midday movement, I still wanted to be in the area at first light. It's a good thing I was — not long after daybreak I looked down the narrow cutline and once again noticed the silhouette of a deer.

I already had my 7mm Rem. Mag. pointing that way, resting on a set of Underwood shooting sticks. Through the scope, I immediately saw the deer was a doe. She was moving nonchalantly along the same trail where I'd seen the doe the previous day. Then, another doe walked out, also picking along without a care. Moments later, they were followed by a third doe, but this one acted far friskier than the others, trotting down the cutline away from me.

Let's see now — peak of the rut and a doe acting suspiciously? Sounded like an impending buck sighting to me, and I stared hard for more movement. Seconds later, I got a scopeful of it when a big-bodied, high-racked buck trotted into view! He moved along purposefully behind that last doe, following in her tracks.

The range was 400 yards or so, and the buck was behind a thin veil of brush the entire time. The shot just wasn't there. I merely gawked through the scope as all four deer melted into the woods again — but not before memorizing the vision of a trophy buck with a high, dark rack and at least one exceptional brow tine.

No doubt the does were moving back to a bedding area after a night of feeding, but I hadn't been here long enough to have any real feel for just where that bedding area was. As is always the case in big woods, the cover was not as uniform as it appeared at first glance. There were pockets of hardwood and softwood regrowth mixed in with the mature timber, and those deer likely were heading to one of those thickets hidden within the forest. Unfortunately, abandoning my makeshift stand and taking off after them wasn't a legal option. An American hunter in Alberta must stay put until his guide returns for him. I saw nothing else but a doe fawn before noon.

Does a full moon result in strictly nocturnal deer activity? No. In fact, during full-moon conditions (the day of the actual full moon, plus a day or two before and after), it's common to see midday movement, as well as short flurries at first and last light. Combine the peak of rut with a full moon and cool to cold weather, and you have a recipe for great buck hunting between 11 a.m. and 2 p.m. — provided, of course, you're not snoozing back in camp.

Being chained to a frigid brushpile while a lovesick trophy buck is stumbling around in the brush only a quarter-mile away is hardly the most pleasant of experiences. This is particularly so when he's the first big deer you've seen in a hard week of hunting, and you know he well could be the last. It's a lot like knowing the exact location of a chest full of Spanish gold on the bottom of the sea but not having a boat!

As is the case with most other laws in western society, the restriction on the movements of American hunters in Alberta woods came in reaction to a perceived problem. In this case, the problem was that in gun season many so-called "outfitters" simply were dropping off their clients wherever they liked before shooting light then driving back into town to hang out at the coffee shop for a few hours. Not surprisingly, some well-meaning clients ended up on posted land, which infuriated landowners and even resident hunters. The subsequent decision to allow American gun hunters to move in the field about only when accompanied by their guides/outfitters no doubt cut down on that problem. But from where I was sitting on that cold Friday morning, hoping the buck would walk back out and blunder into rifle range, that law seemed a pretty extreme way to deal with the problem.

Based on the fact that the buck and does had crossed the cutline at the same place where the second doe had been seen on Thursday afternoon, we decided over lunch that I needed to be within shooting range of the trail. Something had to be going on down there. So, we investigated the scene and learned there were indeed plenty of tracks crossing the cutline right there. No good ground-blind locations stood out, but 75 yards down the cutline from the crossing was a huge, "bull" spruce that towered over the surrounding area. Within a few minutes, we'd used my folding saw to carve out a commanding vantage point some 30 feet off the ground. Now I was ready; let's see Mr. Buck walk across that cutline again!

Every hunter must know his limitations when presented with an opportunity for a shot. The fact that it's getting late in a hunt and you're feeling the pressure of an unfilled tag doesn't make you a better marksman than you otherwise would be. Neither does the sheer size of a buck make a risky shot justifiable. In fact, you often must make a better hit to down a big buck, particularly if he's pumped up from the rut and/or fear. When in doubt, pass up the shot.

He didn't. I sat in the treestand until dark. The only deer I saw was a small doe — probably one of those I'd spotted earlier — that walked behind me in the brush just before sundown. As we drove back to camp that night, I felt we'd made the right moves but hadn't been rewarded. Well, there was still one more day to try.

Waiting for dawn to break on the last day of a tough hunt brings far different feelings than are experienced on opening morning. Then, you were physically fresh and bubbling with confidence; now, your body is worn out and you're frazzled from days of second-guessing yourself. In

A variety of lanes, locally known as "cutlines," slice through the oilfield country of western Alberta. These right-of-ways generally mark the course of pipelines and are excellent places to rattle from or to ambush crossing bucks. Photo by Gordon Whittington.

some ways you just want it all to be over with, for the jury to deliver its verdict, whatever that might be. But then, if you're a serious hunter, you keep telling yourself that you must keep that mental edge, for everything can change in the blink of an eye.

So, as we got dressed on Saturday morning, I was as upbeat as possible, hoping against hope that something good would happen. Just before legal shooting light, I climbed into the nosebleed treestand once again and placed my bet.

Crunch ... crunch ... crunch. I was so high in that black spruce that the sound was faint, but soon after daybreak, I realized a deer was somewhere beneath me. The morning was as still as a corpse. I feared that if I twisted and turned too much in my efforts to spot the animal, I'd make some noise and reveal my position. If that happened, I'd probably not even get a glimpse of the deer. Finally, though, I peered through the boughs and saw that the same young doe (presumably) from the day before was back. She nibbled gray-green moss from a couple of the sawed-off limbs I'd dropped at the base of the tree then walked out of sight in the same direction every other deer on this cutline had gone. I begged for a buck to follow her, but none did.

The minutes turned into hours, and the weight of the hunt really started to work on me. Clearly the prime time for morning movement had passed. Sure, during the rut you can see a big buck at any time of day, but the woods seemed dead now. I found myself wishing for a change of scenery. Maybe I really needed to be somewhere else ... and while I was at it, maybe I needed to try a different tactic. I remembered the grunt call and synthetic rattling antlers in my backpack and wondered if they might be the answer, even though they'd brought in nothing for me all hunt long.

While many hunters prefer to use natural antlers for rattling, the better brands of synthetic antlers will do just as good a job of fooling a buck. One advantage of synthetics is that they tend to be lighter in weight than real antlers of similar size, and thus less of a burden to carry. Also, in cold weather, synthetics don't seem to rob as much heat from a hunter's hands as does real bone.

During the rut in particular, trying to decide where to look for a trophy buck in a vast swamp crisscrossed with cutlines, overgrown roads and an assortment of other small openings is a bit like trying to think of a set of winning lottery numbers. No matter how scientifically you approach it, any ball can fly up the chute at any time ... and a buck can pop out of any piece of woods with as little warning. We were getting down to "crunch time," as they say. There were literally thousands of potentially productive places to hunt here, but only a half-day left in which to select the best one.

On Friday morning, I'd seen that good buck perhaps a half-mile from where Byron had spotted the two bucks months earlier. There was no way of knowing for certain if the deer I'd seen was indeed one of the two he had sighted, or if either of those big bucks were still anywhere around. But when the ship's on fire, you'll take your chances with the sharks. It was time, I figured, to gather up Byron and head straight back to where the two big bucks had been seen in August and September and try to shake things up.

Byron and I walked south, across a wide pipeline right-of-way and then onto a narrow cutline leading farther into the "bush." There, a smattering of fresh deer tracks lifted my spirits a bit. Eventually, the line intersected a wider cutline back in the timber. There were some big rubs along its edge, but they obviously had been made much earlier in the fall. Besides, they were so high on the trees that we knew no whitetail had made them anyway. Most likely a bull elk was to blame, though fresh moose tracks indicated "swamp donkeys" also liked this spot.

The cutline dead-ended into a pine flat to the east and a groaning oil pumpjack perhaps 200 yards to the west. I told Byron that something about it seemed right. He eased back to the vehicle while I crawled into a tangle of spruce roots and let things settle down for maybe five minutes. Then, around 11 a.m., I began my calling routine.

I alternated rattling, grunting and listening for maybe 15 minutes, forcing myself to be patient. Not even a twig moved. But then, just about the time I'd decided nothing was going to show, that little voice told me to check behind one more time.

Turning slowly, I looked into the heavy timber to the south of my position and was stunned to see a big, dark body no more than 20 yards away — and closing!

"If I can get the gun up and shoot this buck before he spots me and blows out of here, it's gonna be the miracle of the century," I recall thinking as the Model 700 Remington floated to my shoulder.

The buck had now stopped walking and was facing me from a distance of no more than 15 yards. Through the scope, my right eye frantically locked in on the best target I could find, a point just beneath the white throat patch. A thin screen of spruce needles was halfway between me and the buck, but I could see his form clearly. I knew a 165-grain bullet screaming along at nearly 3,000 feet per second should have no trouble finding its target through that stuff. This deer was close enough to kill with a spear!

After the recoil of the shot, you can imagine my amazement, then, to discover that no buck was on the ground. He didn't even fall down. He simply gathered himself, turned and ran back into the timber from which he'd just appeared. The spruce branch in front of me was swaying back and forth, but I figured most of that had been caused by the concussion of the magnum's muzzle blast, not by a collision with the bullet. So, why wasn't there a buck lying dead 15 yards from me?

I eased over to where he'd been standing and saw a lot of hair on the ground and on the side of a tree where he'd been standing — but no blood. The hairs were of medium length and dark, as you'd expect of those from the neck area. Most of them were spread out in such a way as to sug-

In heavy cover, the sounds of rattling and grunting don't travel nearly as far as in more open habitat. However, they still can be heard by bucks several hundred yards away, especially on cold, still days. It's critical to give a cautious buck enough time to reach the "fight" scene before you give up on a calling session.

gest the bullet had hit the deer on the right side of his neck, rather than straight on. Could those twigs have deflected the bullet far enough to keep it out of the body cavity? It was hard to imagine, but there was no dead buck here to prove otherwise.

When Byron reached me after the shot, I filled him in on the chaotic events and we pondered the best course of action. Cautiously, we followed the big, running tracks back into the pine flat and on through it toward the main road. Finally, perhaps 100 yards from where the buck had been when I'd fired, we found the first blood — a spray of droplets standing out like tiny rubies on the snow. The blood did indeed seem to be coming from the right side of the deer's body. Not good.

It didn't seem prudent to push the buck farther than he was inclined to go on his own, but the idea of doing nothing was about as appealing as a Spam milkshake. Waiting until dark to round up the rest of the guides and conduct an all-out search for the wounded deer struck me as a bad idea — but then, so did running the deer into a block of "bush" so big and wild that we couldn't possibly catch up to him. Finally, the decision was made: We'd give the buck a little time to lay up then go after him. In the meantime, we'd try to get some help.

There was an oilfield office less than a mile away — with a phone. We headed there and found a friendly young man named Cy O'Malley. We told him our story, and he got on the phone and left word at our camp that all available guides should head our way whenever they got a chance. We might need reinforcements on this one.

Seeing our plight, Cy agreed to help with trailing the buck. As we drove back to the hunting area, we formulated a plan. The trackers were to creep along a few feet off to the side of the deer's trail; I'd circle ahead and set up in the same clearing where that first doe had been seen feeding on Thursday afternoon. If the buck crossed there — and that seemed to be where he was heading — I might get a chance to finish him off.

Soon, I'd eased into position in a spot that would let me see up and down the sizable clearing, which contained a water injector, propane tank and several other assorted pieces of oilfield equipment.

Our plan worked beautifully. Apparently, the buck hadn't gone far before bedding, and he soon was up and heading in my direction. He walked out into the wide open scarcely more than 100 yards from me and stopped, trying to decide which way to go next. I could see he was favoring his right shoulder and that he'd been hit hard. All I had to do was ease my rifle into position, put the crosshairs on him and touch the trigger.

Or so it seemed.

Now, if 100 persons were asked to name 100 objects that might get between a hunter and a trophy whitetail in the wilds of Canada, I'm fairly sure "propane tank" would not show up on any of their lists. But as I swung my rifle around, the wounded buck spotted me and trotted forward several yards — stopping right behind that big, silver tank!

When trailing a wounded deer, either in the snow or on bare ground, always stay off to the side of the trail at least a couple of feet to minimize the chances of disturbing the sign. On many trailing jobs (especially those with little blood and no snow), you might have to backtrack occasionally to the last known sign. You don't want to have destroyed it by careless tromping. This is also the reason that, under most conditions, it's best to have only one person follow the trail and examine blood sign and tracks.

What now? I had my gun up and was fully prepared to shoot the deer when he stepped into the open again, which I assumed would happen at any moment. But several seconds passed, and still no buck. Was he really behind the tank? Or, horror of horrors, had he made a beeline straight away from me into a huge block of timber while hidden by the tank?

Not willing to chance letting him trudge off into the woods without another shot being fired, I came up from my kneeling position, eye still to the scope, slowly raising myself high enough to see over the propane tank. First, a tall rack appeared, then the buck's head and neck, then the top three inches or so of his back. He was broadside, still scarcely more than 125 yards away, looking right at me. As you can imagine, he was antsy. If I was to get a standing shot, it was now or never.

Nobody could have wanted that buck any more than I did. But, I just couldn't figure out how to explain my starting the biggest oilfield fire in Canadian history, which I figured might happen if my offhand shot

Without question, Canada's prairie provinces are home to some of the world's biggest whitetails. A few years before the author's hunt, this mammoth buck was found dead in the nearby farmland area. Photo by Gordon Whittington.

went just a tad low and somehow ignited the propane tank. That kind of stunt would make the captain of the Exxon Valdez look like a choirboy. I held off ... and the buck took off.

Quick now — up to a standing position, get him in the scope, clear the propane tank by a comfortable margin and squeeze off a good shot! I held as best I could on the deer's rump as he was running straight away, now perhaps 175 yards from me. The shot felt good, but he kept motoring into the timber and out of sight.

When we reached the buck's trail, it was apparent that the bullet had indeed hit him. There were more long, dark hairs on the trail, and his tracks showed signs that he had skidded in the snow. A few jumps later, the blood had definitely picked up and we knew he had to be in bad shape. But, should we stay on his trail or await the other guides, who we hoped were now on their way? This time we opted for the latter.

Fortunately for both the buck and my nerves, the end was not much longer in coming. Guides Larry Holman and Richard Fraser arrived only a few minutes later, and we soon found the buck just 300 yards or so back in the timber. He stood and moved shakily out into a small cutline, where a finishing lung shot brought the ordeal to a close. The deer had ended up going a half-mile or so from where I'd rattled him in, even though that initial bullet had in fact gone pretty much where I'd aimed and had sliced through the right lung, just missing the spine en route. The second shot had hit high in the back.

Now, finally, it was time to admire this brute. He was indeed the high racked buck Byron had observed earlier in the year — the smaller of the two — and without question the one I'd seen chasing the doe on Friday morning. His basic 4x4 frame featured a 20 1/2-inch inside spread and tremendous tine length. Each G-2 was pushing 13 inches, while each G-3 was close to 10. And the brow tines were just as strong as I'd thought after that glimpse at 400 yards. The left one measured a solid 5 1/2 inches, and the right one was simply huge, nearly nine inches long and heavily bladed. A three-inch "sticker" off the back of the right G-2 was the only odd point on the rack, which grossed 154 B&C points. We never got a chance to weigh the animal, but he certainly field dressed well over 200 pounds. I later aged him by tooth wear at 4 1/2 years.

It's worth noting that this buck had another interesting feature as well — his left eye had been gouged out not long before, quite possibly in a scrap with his wide-racked buddy in the swamp. Now, I understood why the buck hadn't spooked before I'd first shot him that morning. He'd approached at an angle that had put me in what was literally his "blind spot." He simply hadn't seen me standing in those tree roots until it was too late.

Why had he even come to the rattling and calling? You'd think getting an eye poked out would make a buck somewhat shy about looking for another battle, but not this guy. He should have known, after sustaining such a horrible injury, that violence was waiting for him at the scene of the "buck fight" he was hearing. Yet, after analyzing all of the information his ears were receiving, he somehow settled on the only response that could get him into even more trouble.

I guess that just shows trophy bucks can get brain cramps, too.

Chapter Three

Wyoming's Last-Ditch Whitetail

by Dick Idol

IT WAS STILL PITCH BLACK as I crawled out of Dan's pickup. To the east over the tops of the jagged mountains, I could see a faint glow in the sky, signaling me that it was time to get moving. As I walked around the truck to Dan's window on the driver's side, I was rocked by a blast of wind that forced me to take a side-step to catch my balance.

"Are we expecting some kind of front to hit today?" I asked.

In his best cowboy drawl, Dan replied, "Nope. Blows like this every day."

Grabbing my gun, I headed into the wind and the Wyoming darkness. "Well, I'll see you at 10, if I don't get blown off a cliff!" I was only half-kidding.

As I walked down the "prairie road" — two vague wheel marks through the sagebrush — I kept wondering if Dan was serious. The wind was howling down the hills above me at about 25 or 30 knots, and where I come from, that's a major windstorm. I finally conceded that it didn't really matter. If Dan was telling the truth, the deer were surely accustomed to the wind. At least it would be steady and predictable.

I walked for almost an hour before I finally reached the vantage point I'd located the previous afternoon, a knob that overlooked a sparse alfalfa field along the creek bottom. Earlier in the fall, Dan had seen a massive-racked buck here that he believed might be a "book" deer.

After more conventional tactics failed, the author took his hunt a step further and wound up claiming this huge Wyoming typical. Some abnormal points kept the deer out of the record book, but the great mass of this 14-pointer makes it a spectacular trophy. Photo courtesy of Dick Idol.

I settled in and waited for dawn. As the sky gradually lightened, I watched a horned owl on an old snag silhouetted against the rising sun. It was a picturesque sight, but the wind was giving him a fit. Each time a gust hit him, he'd spread his wings and teeter left and right, struggling to stay on his perch. As I fought the same wind, it struck me that we had a lot in common on this particular day.

That short period each morning, when darkness gradually dissolves into dawn, is perhaps the most magical time of day for a deer hunter. Suspicious forms slowly reveal their true identities, and secrets come to light. Dawn comes slowly in this part of the West, so I had plenty of time to anticipate what might be waiting for me in the alfalfa field. Intently, I glassed the field for deer. There was nothing.

I could hardly believe what my eyes were telling me. Just yesterday, in this same area, I'd seen tracks, trails and big, fresh rubs. How could this be?

By 10 o'clock, I had seen only two does, and both of them were in the brush. I knew from scouting the area that big bucks were frequenting this spot and that they were living in relatively small strips of cover along the main creek drainage and its tributaries. But, I gradually realized that hunting them wouldn't be as easy as I'd thought. I was dealing with extremely nocturnal deer, and my strategy would have to change if I expected to take a trophy buck.

My Wyoming adventure had really begun back in the spring when I was in Sidney, Nebraska, working on a special project for Cabela's. Greg Severinson, who heads the company's booking service for hunting and fishing trips, sauntered into the room where I was working and plopped a big non-typical whitetail rack on the table. Greg and I have been friends for years and have hunted together on many occasions, so he certainly knows how to get my attention. And as always, a big rack is worth a thousand words.

It seems that Greg had just returned from Wyoming where he'd been checking out an outfitter for possible mule deer and antelope hunts. Instead, he suspected that he had stumbled upon a whitetail hotspot. Even though the rack just missed qualifying for the Boone and Crockett record book, its 25-inch spread and 17 points made for an impressive sight. I'm sure I was bug-eyed as I admired the antlers in a way that only a whitetail nut could appreciate.

Greg just watched me. He knew I'd have to ask.

Finally I said, "Well, what's the story?"

A sneaky grin crossed his face. "This one came from that ranch last season."

There was another long pause. I could see that he was going to make me work at this.

"Have they taken anything else good off the ranch?" I inquired.

He looked at me with a stone face. "Four hunters killed four bucks about like this one last season," he said matter-of-factly.

That was all I could take. "Okay," I begged. "Give me the whole story. And who do I have to kill to get on this hunt?" The next thing I

In this photograph, taken later near the author's home, it's easy to appreciate the 26-inch-plus main beams. The buck had a 22-inch spread, and some tines were more than 12 inches long. Photo courtesy of Dick Idol.

knew, I was one of eight hunters booked for the 1987 season.

If there was anything that bothered me about this hunt, it was that it actually sounded too good! Four hunters last season had all taken big bucks? I've heard lots of these hard-to-believe success stories before and have learned that most of them are characterized by a strong "essence of bull." But in this case, my apprehension was relieved when I spoke by telephone to Dan Artery, the outfitter for the hunt.

Dan and his partner, Lee Miller, both live in Wheatland, Wyoming, and make a living farming wheat and doing a little outfitting. I could tell from his low-key demeanor during our conversation that he was a straight-

The author's trophy buck was hiding in this patch of sunken willows located far from any other cover in a bend in the creek bottom. A last-minute push through the unlikely looking spot forced the deer out of its lair. Photo by Dick Idol.

shooter and knew what he was talking about. He didn't claim to be the greatest outfitter in the world, but he knew big bucks. He was certain there were more like the one Greg had shown me on his lease. And the four hunters from last year? He told me that two of their deer had grossed the book but their net scores had fallen barely short. The other two bucks netted in the 150s and 160s. By now, I was fully charged and could hardly wait for October.

At the time, this part of Wyoming had a split season, with 10-day gun seasons in October and November. I opted to apply for the earlier season, and fortunately, I was successful on the draw.

Because of my fascination with deer hunting, I try to pay close attention to regions producing exceptional whitetails. Eastern Wyoming is primarily known for antelope and mule deer, but in recent years, there had been more and more stories of big whitetail bucks in the area. The whitetails are relatively new to the region, meaning that they are in the process of occupying a territory where they've never existed before. Invariably, these sorts of emerging populations produce some monster bucks.

As the season arrived, I found myself driving from a deer show in South Dakota to my long-awaited hunt. Along the way I passed through some beautiful country, but it was undoubtedly mule deer/antelope terrain. There was a distinct lack of trees and an abundance of prairie and sagebrush. Even though I had complete confidence in the reports I'd been given, this certainly seemed like unlikely whitetail country. The fact that I saw numerous mulies and antelope, but no whitetails, didn't boost my confidence.

After Dan and I exchanged introductions in Wheatland, we drove along 40 miles of gravel roads to reach our camp located within their 75,000 acres of leased hunting land. The camp was a spruced-up old farmhouse nestled high among the sage-covered hills. Not only was it a comfortable setting, but we could watch big mulie bucks right from the yard.

Three of the other four hunters in camp were guys I'd hunted with before — Sam Wyatt, Larry Keenan and Steve Reichard. The last hunter, Homer, would be arriving a day late. The usual late-night "bull session" soon had us all worked up to a fever pitch.

After my opening-morning experience, which featured lots of wind and no deer, we began to analyze our situation more carefully. Because the rut appeared to be at least a month away and deer movement was minimal, we decided that deer drives may be our best tactic, especially during the midday periods.

While does hold the key to buck movement during the rut, early season bucks are influenced more by food than by sex. As a result, these deer won't travel very far in daylight hours; they tend to bed down close to their feeding areas; and they are much more nocturnal than rutting deer. Consequently, hunters generally need to hunt very close to bedding areas or use some kind of forced drive to create movement.

The decision to try deer drives was prompted mainly by the terrain. From the ranch house to the creek bottoms in our hunting area, it was an hour drive across washed-out roads, through wire gates and cattle guards and across rough gullies. It was classic mule deer terrain, characterized by "tall hills" or "low mountains" (depending upon where you're from) and covered with high, dense sagebrush often six to eight feet tall. In much of the West's mule deer country, deer tend to retreat into the steep crags of the high country. But here, the exceptionally tall sagebrush serves as the primary cover. These deer could vanish simply by walking into this stuff!

As you drop down from these hills, an altogether different habitat appears — one which looks a lot more like "typical" whitetail range. Here, large strips of cottonwood trees are strung along the wet creek drainage. At some places, the tree band is 200 yards wide, but at others it dwindles down to nothing, leaving only wide-open prairie. Although the creek meanders through a wide, flat valley floor, the only real cover exists along the fringes of the drainage. On either side of the cover are several hundred yards of relatively flat prairie. Beyond this are the hills, tall sagebrush and rough ravines that serve as secondary cover for pressured whitetails that are pushed out of the creek bottoms.

The terrain often can have a great impact on your choice of hunting tactics. For example, narrow strips of trees or brush, small woodlots, willow stands or tall weed patches are examples of cover that are difficult to hunt. This is especially true when deer are bedding within them, because whitetails often rest just inside the fringes and keep a close watch over the open countryside. Stand-hunting is difficult because an undetected approach is nearly impossible. Also, deer in these situations realize their vulnerability and tend to be much more nocturnal than whitetails living in areas of heavy cover. Deer drives, then, become the logical tactic. The downside, however, is that when bucks are pushed from this cover, they tend to run long distances and often do not return to the same cover for days, becoming very difficult to relocate.

In areas such as this with little cover, hunting can be tough because deer tend to be more nocturnal. But on the other hand, smaller patches of cover provide good settings for deer drives. In this case, it was critical that we be successful on our drives the first time, because these bucks almost always "headed for the hills" once they were spooked. And when they disappeared into that rough terrain and tall sagebrush, there was no way to find them. Once pushed out of their haunts, those deer wouldn't return to the creek bottoms for several days, at least not during the daytime.

After Dan picked me up at 10 o'clock that first morning, we drove 12 miles south to meet the other guys, who were hunting on a new lease. Those hunters also had watched from strategic vantage points at daybreak hoping to spot a good buck but hadn't seen anything. Although the area looked good and a lot of deer were obviously using a big alfalfa field along the edge of some cottonwoods, neither Dan nor Lee had spied any big bucks in the area.

So for the rest of the day, we pushed six miles of creek bottom on this new lease but didn't see any outstanding bucks, or any sign from big deer. By the end of the day, we concluded that while there were numerous bucks here, the likelihood of finding a trophy was very slim. One shot was taken at a decent buck as he high-tailed it away from us, but he escaped untouched. It was a frustrating outing.

Now there were only four days left to hunt, and the weather had turned hot, even for mid-October. With the peak of the rut still weeks away, deer activity was likely to remain slow. We decided to escalate our plans for pushing the deer.

On the second morning, I returned to the same spot I'd watched the first day, but there was very little deer activity and no good bucks. At 8:30, Dan picked me up and we headed out to check with the other guys. No one had seen anything noteworthy.

This day, however, we planned to do some pushes on the previous year's lease, where Dan had seen some good bucks earlier in the fall. Because of the wind direction and the threat of other hunting pressure on the south end of the lease, we decided to begin there and work our way north.

To set up our drives, we positioned a hunter on each outside edge of the cover. These two men would stay even with, or walk slightly ahead of, the drivers who pushed through the middle of the cover. This way, the outside hunters could watch for any bucks that tried to escape from the sides. At the same time, we posted hunters at any natural openings in the cover where deer would be likely to head. We worked our way north all morning using this strategy, tackling segments of the creek bottom that extended anywhere from a quarter-mile to a full mile in length. By late afternoon, we had covered four miles of bottomland but still hadn't seen any really good bucks. Because the creek was lined with heavy clumps of willows, tall weeds and thick brush, it was quite possible that the bucks were slipping back through the drivers or were holding tight as the men passed. At least we knew the bucks were there, because we were beginning to find some big rubs.

Finally, we reached one of the largest patches of cottonwoods in the area, which seemed sure to hold some big bucks. We had been rotating positions, and on this drive, Steve, Larry and I were posted while Sam

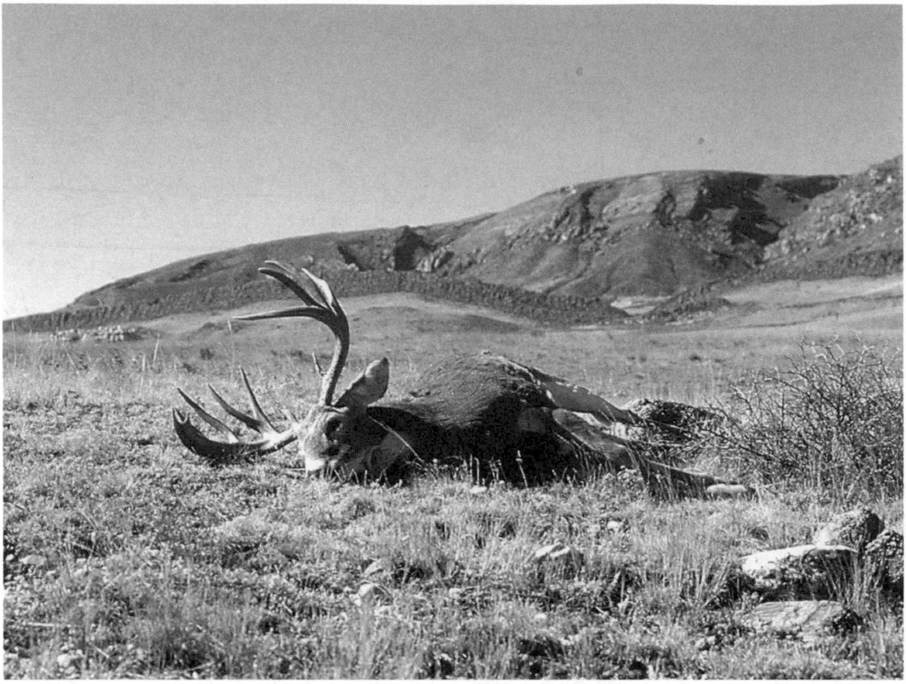

As the big whitetail bolted from its cover and headed cross-country, the author used four shots to bring him down. The buck stopped here, 300 yards from the willow thicket where he'd been bedded. Photo by Dick Idol.

walked along the edge.

First, the other standers and I walked for half a mile so we could get into position without disturbing the deer. It seemed like hours before I heard the first distant "whoops" of the drivers. Within minutes, I saw flashes of deer through the cottonwoods as the animals moved toward the end of the cover. Just then, Sam, who had moved ahead of the drivers, walked into the opening directly across from my position, kneeling as soon as he saw me. He essentially had positioned himself between Larry and me, and I could already sense that a problem was brewing.

Within minutes, five deer — including one good buck — broke from the timber and headed toward Larry. I couldn't shoot because of Sam, so I watched them disappear. Seconds later, I heard Sam fire three shots, but I had no way to tell if he'd been successful. Silence followed.

We had decided earlier that every stander would hold his position, regardless of whether or not he'd fired a shot, until all the drivers had finished. It was a full five minutes before I heard a shot from Larry. I was puzzled because I could see the general area and I hadn't seen any other deer. Five more minutes passed and another shot was fired from the same area, but again, I saw no deer.

It wasn't until later that I learned the entire scenario. As it turned out, the first trio of shots were Sam killing the same buck I'd watched cross the opening in front of us. But, the story behind the next shot was more bizarre.

Whenever you stage deer drives or try to force deer movement, don't be fooled into thinking that whitetails are always (or even usually) going to move in the desired direction. Generally, when bucks figure out which way a drive is moving, they'll use every trick in the book to circle behind the drivers. Expect bucks to do the unexpected, especially the big ones.

Larry, it seems, had been standing for more than an hour only 20 yards from the edge of the creek. When Sam shot his buck, the deer fell within 40 yards of Larry. No one moved. Five minutes later, another buck — which had been bedded 20 yards from Larry the entire time — suddenly jumped up from the cover and Larry killed him at point-blank range. The last shot? That came when Sam saw just how big his buck really was. He fired a "make-sure" round for good measure.

When the drivers came out of the trees, I heard yelling and presumed someone had killed something. But, I hadn't expected to see two big bucks resting 40 yards apart! Sam's trophy was a huge non-typical that measured 23 inches wide and had 17 points. But, the most unique feature was the giant palmated, "caribou-like" point coming up on the inside of the left main beam. Larry had taken a huge 8-pointer whose rack was 23 inches wide with 6-inch bases. Finally, we'd hit pay dirt.

On the third day, we continued to work north along the creek bottom using the same tactics. Homer, our late-arriving hunter, took a heavy-beamed, 20-inch 10-pointer late in the day, meaning that only Steve and I remained for the last two days. Somehow, it seems like I'm always in this situation!

By the fourth day, we had reached the last three or four miles of untouched creek bottom. During the previous three days, I'd watched here nearly every morning and evening, trying to get a glimpse of the buck Dan had seen earlier. So far, though, I hadn't seen a single good buck in this spot. But, that had also been the case where we'd taken the good bucks previously, so I knew that not seeing any deer didn't mean they weren't there. I was concerned, however, by the fact that a bowhunter had been hunting a big buck here earlier and may have pushed the animal into the sagebrush hills. Was the buck's activity completely nocturnal or had he moved to another area? That is often the classic question when it comes to finding big bucks, and I had only two more days to find the answer.

One of the great lessons to be learned by any deer hunter is that "it ain't over 'til it's over!" On many hunts, I've seen guys become progressively more depressed when they weren't having the same success that other hunters were enjoying. This attitude can prevent a hunter from staying alert, prepared and enthusiastic. Then, when an opportunity does arise, the hunter isn't ready. Remember, the complexion of any hunt can change in seconds, and at any moment, your hunt may evolve from a bitter failure into a great success.

By the fourth and next-to-last day of the hunt, we headed for a strip of creek bottom I'd been hunting all week. We had already done drives everywhere else, and now we realized that there would be virtually no deer movement at all unless we forced it. The hunt was headed for a showdown, and it was obvious that if anything at all was going to happen, we would have to make it happen.

After almost a week of pushing brush, we knew that we had been victimized by some "Houdini-like" escape acts. Judging from the fresh buck sign we were finding, it was obvious that we still hadn't seen a substantial portion of the big buck there. Some undoubtedly had escaped out the sides early in the drive and headed for the hills. Others had probably cut back through the drivers and simply vanished. And I'm sure many more hunkered down in their beds and let the drivers walk by. We even caught some deer getting into the water in the creek so they could circle back. With just Steve and myself remaining as hunters, I realized our odds were dwindling.

On the first drive, we pushed to the north and I saw a couple of good bucks, but not what I was hoping for. Steve and I again posted on the second push, still working north, and this time I had a long look at a tempting buck. He was a solid 21-inch, basic 8-pointer with a long kicker point and 13-inch back tines. I even put the crosshairs on him as he stood broadside at 40 yards. Finally, he'd had enough and broke past me in a steady run, heading for the big hills. I was relieved when he ended my temptation.

But before long, I began talking to myself. After all, we had just pushed the strips where I thought I'd find "the big one," and I'd come out empty-handed. Perhaps I should have taken the 8-pointer after all. But, it was too late to second-guess.

We now had reached the last stretch of creek bottom, and our last hope. Steve would be the lone stander because the narrow open gap could be easily covered by one hunter. I would flank the pushers on the east side in case anything broke for the hills.

For some reason, this area had few deer, and we'd seen no bucks at all here in the past week. When we reached the end of the drive, I could see Steve ahead of me and all the drivers below. Mostly due to habit, we stayed in formation as we continued to walk both sides of the creek, trudging the final 200 yards through wide-open prairie. No one had seen anything. When we reached Steve's position, I peered past him to where some willow tops were barely protruding above the banks of the creek about 50 yards away. For some reason, I knew I had to take a look.

In my experience, successful deer hunts rarely happen exactly the way you envision them. Luck often plays a role, but you have to put yourself in position to be lucky. The more time you spend in an area known to hold a big buck, the more you stack the odds in your favor. We may never know exactly where, when or how our chance will arise, but we can keep exposing ourselves to those chances.

I passed within a few feet of Steve and continued walking toward the willow tops.

"Where are you going?" asked Steve.

"Just sit tight for a minute," I replied, never breaking stride. "I'm going to check out these willows."

By now, he must have thought I was completely crazy. He'd been sitting within 50 yards of those willows for two hours, and five or six guys were milling around and talking, all within a 100-yard circle. We were in the middle of a flat, 300-yard stretch of creek bottom with virtually no cover except a little strip that hugged the sunken creek bed, and that strip was just 10 to 20 yards wide and 15 to 20 feet below ground level. Beyond this speck of cover was nothing but open prairie. On top of that, on the second push of the day, the drivers had started their march within 50 yards of this same bend in the creek. But some nagging inner voice kept telling me to check it out, because this was the only 50 yards of creek bottom in a four-mile stretch that we hadn't pushed that day.

Lee, who was the only driver remaining on the opposite side of the creek, alertly realized what I was doing and began angling toward the same point. As we both approached the creek bank, he looked down over the edge and saw a buck rise to its feet among the thick willows below. Suddenly, I heard the crash of antlers and knew that a big buck was about to burst out of the cover somewhere. Finding myself standing among a series of small, rugged hills, I darted to the top of the highest hump, hoping to gain a good vantage point.

Big whitetail bucks are notorious for sizing up hunting pressure and then reacting accordingly. How that hunting pressure is applied will determine every aspect of a buck's travel pattern. In the case of my Wyoming buck, I feel sure the bowhunter who had been hunting him earlier probably was stand-hunting in the strips of cover on either side of where I discovered him. The open bottom between these strips was more than likely the only area not disturbed by that hunter. That's why the buck chose it. The lesson? Look for pockets and seams that other hunters overlook—and be ready.

Just as I topped the hill, the buck leaped up from the creek bottom and bolted to the crest of a 10-foot vertical dirt bank, stopping behind a heavy-limbed tree to get his bearings. I fired once through a tiny opening, grazing his shoulder, but he didn't flinch or fall. Instead, he dashed for the hills. After three more shots, the final one coming at about 300 yards, he was down for good.

When the smoke cleared, everyone in the group seemed stunned. No buck in his right mind should have been bedded here, yet this one almost got away with it. He had let people walk past him all day, and his nerve held until he was practically kicked out of his bed.

It had been worth the wait. He was a great buck, with a 22-inch spread and 14 points. His beams were both over 26 inches long, and some tines stretched upward more than 12 inches. Near the ends of both beams he was heavily palmated, and he sported a deep fork in his right G-2 point. When measured, he grossed just under 180 Boone and Crockett typical points but netted in the low 160s. Without doubt, he was one of the best bucks I'd ever taken.

Sam Wyatt's huge non-typical taken on a drive earlier in the hunt was 23 inches wide with 17 points. It has a distinctive palmated point on the inside of its left beam. Photo by Dick Idol.

Wyoming had been good to me. This hunt had been fun, the weather mild, and I'd taken a great buck. Some of the other guys also connected on great mulie bucks measuring 25 to 30 inches wide. You couldn't ask for more.

But in many ways, this was a strange and contradictory hunt. True, we constantly saw big mulie bucks, antelope and other game generally associated with this part of the West. And the pungent smell of prairie sage, the ever-present cactus and sand spurs and that persistent Wyoming wind made it feel more like an antelope hunt. But even in this somewhat alien land, the whitetails had remained true to their nature. In their own isolated niche, they were still as elusive as ever, and they had again proved their adaptability by making this prairie environment their own.

Whitetails, I had learned, will always be whitetails, no matter where they live!

CHAPTER FOUR

A Buck For The Old Guys

by Bob Haney

LYING AWAKE IN THE DARKNESS, I struggled to remember. Somewhere in the past, lost in my distant memories, were the clues I needed. The "old guys" had spent years preparing me for this moment. But now, I was on my own — searching for a plan and running out of time.

If only I could talk with Grandpa and his old hunting buddies one more time. I'd ask them what to do, what mistakes to avoid, what tactic to try. During all those nights around the fireplace when Grandpa was telling us his hunting stories, he also had been teaching me how to be a deer hunter. In years of hunting together, he'd taught me a lifetime's worth of skills. Tonight, I needed to remember them all: I couldn't afford a single mistake if I was going to outwit the awesome buck that had eluded me all season.

Staring at the ceiling through the darkness of my bedroom, I resigned myself to another sleepless night. My mind replayed everything that had happened. I had been so close, but I'd failed. Now, I feared I'd never see the buck again, or someone else would take him before I'd get another chance. This wasn't just any buck. The whitetail I'd glimpsed twice before was unlike any I'd ever seen. He could well be one of the biggest ever in Ohio — a buck so immense he seemed unreal. Just thinking about him made it impossible to sleep, and rekindled the same excitement and wonder I'd known as a boy.

With main beams exceeding 29 inches and back tines surpassing 15 inches, the author's whitetail is the biggest 8-pointer ever taken with a bow. The Ohio giant scored 180 1/8 B&C points as a typical and 196 5/8 as a non-typical, making the record book either way. Photo courtesy of Bob Haney.

Back then, my Grandpa and the "old guys" all worked in the steel mill. I couldn't wait for him to come home from work each evening and build a fire in the fireplace. After dinner, while I sat on Grandpa's lap beside that roaring fire, he'd thrill me with story after story. Only four or five years old, I listened in awe as he described every detail of some far-away hunt. He had a lifetime of stories and knowledge, and he tried to share it all with me. The tone of his voice and the sparkle in his eyes made me feel like I was there, too. I ached to grow up quickly so I could be a deer hunter just like him.

It started at age six, with my first BB gun. By eight, I had moved up to a .22 rifle and a shotgun. Fortunately, hunting was a part of our family; when Dad and Grandpa had to work, Mom took me small-game hunting. Still, I spent each day waiting for my chance to go deer hunting. I just couldn't get big enough, fast enough.

Every year, usually on the first chilly fall evening, the phone would ring, and it would be one of the "old guys" asking Grandpa to come to the deer meeting. Those meetings consisted of 8 to 10 guys who worked at the mill together and who shared a common bond of whitetail hunting. Each November, the group would go hunting together in places like Quebec, Maine or Pennsylvania. I called them the "old guys" because, at my tender age, 50 to 60 years old was really old.

The meeting was always held at the tractor barn on a dairy farm. When it was cold outside, a lively fire danced in the black potbelly stove. The "old guys" gathered around on stumps, drinking coffee and making pitches for their favorite destinations. I absorbed every word spoken by these "gods" of the deer hunt. They knew everything! Best of all, they never tired of my constant questions. So, imagine my surprise when, at age 12, the "old guys" asked Grandpa to let me come hunting that year! Grandpa acted surprised, but I'm sure he was in on it.

For the next 10 years, we hunted all over the U.S. and Canada. I learned different approaches and tactics, as well as some personal "secrets" from each man. I'm still grateful for all the patience, wisdom and guidance they gave me as a boy.

Sadly, time caught up with each and every one of them. When Grandpa died, the woods became a quiet, lonely place. I lost all interest in hunting. Soon I was married and immersed in my work. When the economy slowed in Ohio, we moved to Texas. As time went on, the pain of my loss became more bearable and the woods began to call me back. I realized that all the time and effort expended by the "old guys" had really been an investment, both in me and in the sport. I didn't want to let go of hunting, and I didn't want to let down the men who had taught me.

We moved back to Ohio and fixed up the summer cabin Grandpa had built in the 1950s. Right from the start, I began watching deer around the cabin and practicing with my bow. The feelings were coming back! I subscribed to all the deer hunting magazines and digested every word. When I saw Ronnie Osborne and his huge Ohio non-typical buck on the cover of *North American WHITETAIL* magazine, I decided to meet him. When I did, I discovered that he was a regular guy, like me. But, he plant-

When the author killed his huge whitetail, the deer was traveling from the large stand of oaks and maples (on the right) through the "transition zone" of small trees (on the left). During the day, deer avoided the open soybean field in the foreground. Photo by Bob Haney.

ed a new seed, something the "old guys" hadn't taught me. Because we had always hunted different areas each year, we never pursued one particular buck. But, Ron made me realize that if I wanted to shoot a really big whitetail, I would have to apply everything I knew about deer hunting to taking a single buck.

In the fall of 1987, I told my wife, Joni, that I was going to hold out for a big buck like I saw in the magazines. Because I lived less than 10 miles from where Ron Osborne took his big non-typical, I figured there had to be another one like that around. By the time the season started, I had received written permission to hunt about 700 total acres on various farms. I watched a number of deer around the cabin all summer, but no big boys. The early part of the season I spent scouting, because that's the most difficult time to bowhunt.

By the first of November, sign was showing up everywhere. The rut was going full blast, and I was seeing deer daily. Having spotted plenty of significant sign on my own land, I decided to concentrate on finding the buck that had made it. One day as I still-hunted through the area, I was shocked to find three-inch pines shredded right to the ground! On top of that, several oaks as big around as my leg were showing damage from heavy rubbing. This sign was smoking hot, and I proceeded to locate a stand right away.

At 20 acres, the area I was hunting is relatively small. It's a transition zone between two large hardwood stands, and it contains a small creek, tall grass and medium-sized oaks and pines. About 35 yards from the sign I'd located, I spied a good-sized oak that had been blown into a pine by heavy winds. It was perfect. I climbed up the oak and into the pine, about 15 feet off the ground.

Deer know their home territory intimately. If you change something in their surroundings, they're liable to grow suspicious and avoid the area. For that reason, I carry fishing line with me to tie back branches that may be in my way. When I leave, the limbs go back in their place, reducing any sign of an intrusion.

After pulling up my equipment, I took some monofilament line out of my fanny pack and tied back just enough limbs to allow me to draw my bow and shoot without interference. I remembered the "old guys" stressing that natural stands were the best, and this perch sure beat dragging in a man-made stand and disturbing everything. After installing my safety belt on the pine, I sat back and enjoyed my vantage point. For hours I watched, lost in the memories of previous hunts. Soon it was that magical time of the day when the light fades, the moon starts to rise and animals begin to stir.

Out of the corner of my eye, I saw movement. As I turned my head, I slowly reached for my bow. A huge set of antlers was moving through the trees! The buck's body blended in so well with the dark oaks that I had to look through my binoculars to be sure it wasn't some kind of apparition. The mass and size of its rack were breathtaking. But, there was no chance to shoot — he was at least 50 yards out. Then he vanished. My mind went into overdrive. Did he see me? Smell me? Had he noticed me pick up my bow or binoculars? Was he lurking in the shadows, watching me at this very moment?

I was afraid to move. The last thing I wanted was to alert him to my presence. I just sat there; frozen, listening, waiting. About 30 minutes after blackness had settled in, I gathered the courage to make my escape from his domain. I knew I had to leave as slowly and quietly as possible.

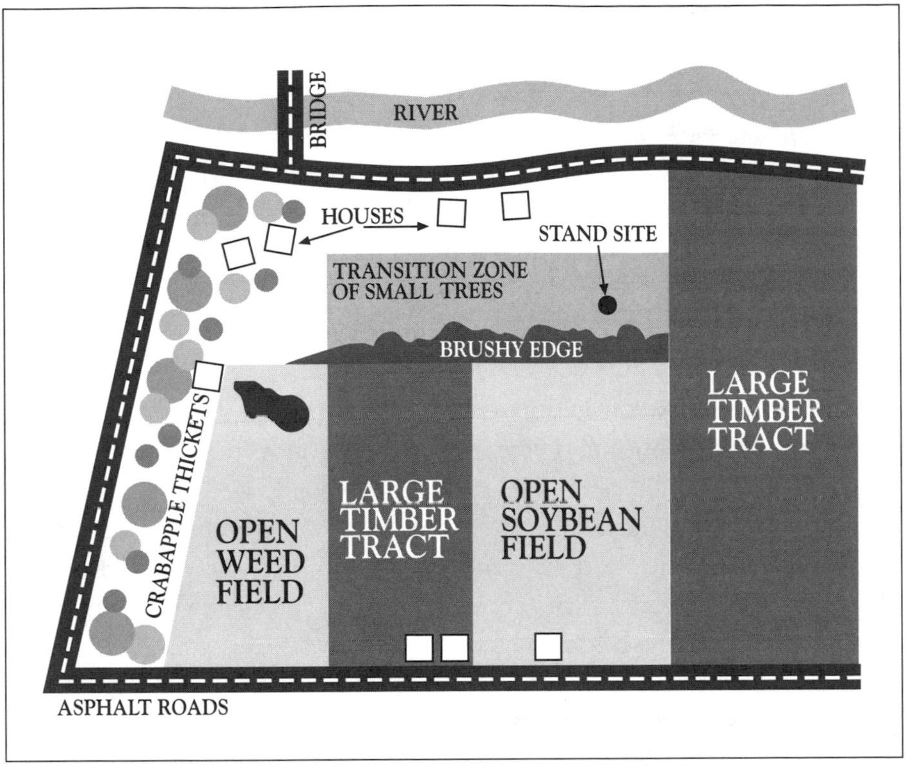

The author realized that bucks from two large timber tracts refused to cross the open weed field or soybean field during daylight hours and counted on them moving through the "transition zone" that linked those two hideouts. This stretch of small trees, ringed by brush and thickets, proved to be a travel corridor for one of the greatest 8-pointers ever.

Taking off my belt and lowering my bow created sounds that seemed deafening. It's amazing how excitement can heighten your senses. Inch by inch, I made my way down, then gently tiptoed out of the woods.

The actual sighting had lasted less than 10 seconds, but I had seen enough. This was the buck I'd dreamed about. During the long walk home, ideas whirled through my head. First, I knew I couldn't tell anyone about him. Even the slightest pressure or intrusion would affect my chances of seeing him again. Secondly, I began to appreciate the magnitude of what I had just witnessed. This was the greatest of whitetails, and it was solely up to me to carry on the tradition of fair chase passed on by Grandpa and the "old guys." To claim such a magnificent buck, especially with a bow and arrow, would be a tribute to their memories. I badly wanted that buck, for myself and for Grandpa.

In my heart, I knew the chances of seeing him again were mighty slim but welcomed the challenge. I began formulating a game plan. Actually, there were a number of points in my favor. For one, Ohio has a very liberal archery season, usually 120 days long, so I had until the end of January to reach my goal. The cabin is located in Mahoning County, in northeast Ohio, where the terrain is basically hardwoods interspersed with small farm tracts. Most of the timber stands average 60 to 100 acres in size, while the fields between these stands usually contain corn or soybeans.

Because the cabin is situated on a river between Lakes Berlin and Milton, water is plentiful. There are numerous farm ponds and swamps, ranging from 10 to 40 acres. The swamps are usually wet, thick and nasty enough to hide big bucks year after year. Most Ohio archers ignore these jungles and concentrate their stand sites around food sources. However, the terrain is so diverse, with acorns and food crops everywhere, it can be difficult to choose the best stand location.

The area where I saw the monster buck is what I call a transition zone. It's basically a grown-up field with medium-sized trees that separates two stands of mature timber. This old field is about 20 acres in size with a brushy edge bordering the big timber. Due south of the 20 acres is about a 90-acre stand of mature oaks and maples that stretches 500 yards wide. The east border of this stand is a large soybean field. The west side is a large field overgrown with weeds and holding a 15-acre stock pond. Bucks don't like to cross either of these big fields in daylight hours. They prefer to go north and travel the brushy edge on my property.

The presence of human scent always means danger to deer. Every piece of your clothing or equipment should be kept scent-free and away from sources of contamination. Before entering the woods, spray yourself with some type of human scent control. Don't depend on these cover scents alone, though; you still need to be clean and free of any odor, and downwind of the deer if at all possible.

I found myself totally bewildered. I couldn't figure out which approach to use, but there were a few certainties. First, I had to be as clean and scent-free as possible. Second, the wind would have to be right, or I couldn't hunt. Also, noise and movement had to kept to an absolute minimum. And one more thing: Any error on my part and the game could be over.

But what strategy should I use? The experts I'd read had taught me to vary my stand sites, use a grunt call, make mock scrapes, rattle with big horns, cut wide shooting lanes and dozens of other lessons. Was I confused? You bet. But after a few days of mental anguish, I finally got it together.

The master plan was simple. I had to shower right before each hunt, and all my equipment had to be scent-free. I normally wore rubber boots, but for this buck I'd change to hip boots to further reduce any scent. I began practicing constantly, pounding targets with broadheads from an elevated stand. A single shot would be crucial, and I had to be sure I could make it.

I was gambling that I had found the right place to ambush the buck, and I felt confident. After all, I had actually seen him walking here, and it was the size and concentration of those huge rubs that had led me to the area in the first place. I didn't really understand why this spot was so attractive to him, but there was no doubt he was spending a lot of time and energy here. I reasoned it would be foolish to go blundering around the woods searching for his bedding or core area. That could spook him out of the area and leave too much human scent. No, it was better like this. No one else seemed to be hunting him; I hadn't even heard anyone mention seeing a deer like this. The natural blind, I believed, was my best choice.

All types of scents must be used properly and at the right time. If the whitetails are keyed in on food sources, use food scents like apple or acorn. Sex scents should be used only when sign or activity indicates that bucks are near or in the rut. Using sex scents early or late in the season will create an unnatural situation that will alarm deer.

The next few weeks, I hunted exactly as I had planned. Every second I spent in that tree blind, my senses were on full alert. I was so intent and focused that nothing in the woods escaped my gaze. I saw does, small bucks, foxes and squirrels, but no monster buck. Soon, my entire life seemed to be wrapped up in this place. At work, I counted the minutes until I could return to my stand. When I spotted new sign and rubs, it just heightened my enthusiasm. The rut came and went without a single sight-

This is the area where the author took his 1987 Ohio trophy — a 20-acre stretch of small trees that connects two larger tracts of mature timber. Rubs and scrapes helped him pinpoint a good location for his stand. Photo by Bob Haney.

ing of the big one, however, and I passed up excellent shots at smaller bucks. Still, I kept at it. I realized, though, that my hunt was actually becoming an addiction.

Then came the second sighting. It was Thanksgiving. Family doings and the big dinner kept me home until about 2:30 that afternoon, when I crept into the woods once again. After almost four weeks without a sighting, I decided to throw the dice. My natural setup thus far had been unsuccessful, so I tried something bold and unnatural.

I placed several scent canisters filled with buck lure in front of my stand in the only area where I had a path to shoot. I knew the big whitetail would never tolerate another buck in his area. Perhaps if he smelled the scent, he would come to me. It was a little risky, but you can sit there like a statue for only so long. From previous experiments with scents, I knew they could attract deer that might otherwise go unseen. It was worth a try.

At 4 p.m., I spotted movement as three does cautiously approached along the brushy strip. They were exceptionally skittish, but I attributed that to the large number of small-game hunters who were out hunting that day. The does' bobbing heads and constant sniffing told me they had detected the scent. Nervously watching their backtrail, they didn't linger around the scent canisters, but kept moving.

By the way the does were acting, I expected to see another hunter show up. I was wrong — it was the monster buck! There was no mistaking those thick main beams and long tines that were now headed straight at me. Somehow I managed to get my bow at full draw. No mistakes now! Concentrate. He grunted and moved closer to my tree. My only thought was to find an opening to shoot, and locate the aiming point. Don't look at the antlers!

But I held up. I couldn't attempt a shot. The many hours of practice had boosted my confidence, but also had taught me the limitations of my equipment. Even the smallest of limbs, I knew, would deflect the arrow off course. I had left everything natural around my stand, and now, I couldn't find a clear path for the 30-yard shot I was facing. The adrenaline that had kept my bow at full draw suddenly seemed to melt away, and so did the deer.

Shooting lanes are open areas near a stand where a bowhunter can make a clear shot. To stay as concealed as possible, I prefer to have only one lane directly in front of the stand. I simply tie back the tree limbs far enough so that I have room to draw my bow and shoot. I've seen hunters cut everything down to the ground around their stands. Leave it as you found it, and you'll see more deer.

I was physically drained as I collapsed against the pine in disbelief. Though frustrated almost to tears, I knew I had done the right thing. Taking a risky shot at a walking deer was something I just couldn't do. I'd been taught too many times to honor the animal, and never compromise your ethics. Besides, I knew I wasn't alone in the woods. Somewhere out there, a bunch of "old guys" was watching. I couldn't disappoint them.

For the first time, my confidence was slipping as I walked back to the cabin, the longest walk I'd ever made. With gun season starting next week, I knew this was probably my final opportunity to take the big buck. No hunter could miss seeing those huge antlers running through the woods. I just knew my buck would show up one day at a deer check station or in the newspaper, shot by a neophyte hunter who had blundered into him.

My attitude the next few days was horrendous. Joni knew something was seriously wrong, and she kept asking until I spilled the terrible story. While she didn't know very much about deer hunting, she did know me, and she helped stop my emotional slide. "You've shot lots of bucks," she said. "This big one is a deer just like them. You can't give up. You're not a quitter."

I vowed to keep trying. Sleep didn't come easily, and I would toss and turn at night, thinking about the big buck. Every day after work, I cruised by the deer check stations to see if he'd been brought in. I felt elation when he wasn't there, but fear that he'd be taken the next day. What a roller coaster of emotions! I'd stay at the station every day until the last hour, watching each vehicle that rolled in. I had to know. Finally, the last day came and no one had shot the big buck. He was still there! It was time for a new plan.

After replaying the first two encounters in my mind for the millionth time, I decided something must be wrong with my setup. I knew he had smelled the canisters, but it bothered me that he didn't come closer. The oak that leaned into my pine tree, I realized, had fallen just last month. Perhaps the deer weren't comfortable with it yet. I made up my mind to move closer to where the deer had been standing.

That meant putting up a stand, but the only one I owned was a humongous climbing-type stand, which happened to be both old and noisy. I had no confidence at all that I could use it successfully. That buck could be in the next county and still hear me putting it up. A new, lightweight portable stand was on my Christmas list, but that was three weeks away. Unknown to me, however, Joni had put in a call to Santa, and they had decided to ship it early. Never has there been a better gift, or one delivered with better timing.

Sneaking back into the woods, I put up the new stand in the only pine tree that was closer to where the buck had walked. I still refused to cut anything out of the way, trying to keep the site as unchanged as possible. My next chance to hunt would be on Saturday, December 12. I was anxious, but also fearful that the gun season might have disrupted his travel patterns.

At 5 a.m. that Saturday, I poured a cup of coffee in my kitchen and checked outside. A stiff blast of cold air reminded me that winter was arriving. Windy weather usually meant little or no deer movement, but at least the wind was blowing in the right direction. It was 35 degrees, with

Scent drags are scent-free pieces of cloth to which you apply deer scents. By attaching them to a two-foot monofilament line dragging from your boots, you can create a mock trail. Never let the scent actually get on you or your boots. With scent pads, on the other hand, you often wind up with some scent on the bottoms of your boots. I've had deer follow me to my stand enough times to realize this can be a problem, because I don't want a deer to know where I'm sitting.

not a star in the sky. Not ideal conditions, but they would have to do.

I vowed to stick to my plan, even when it started to drizzle. I knew the wind would cover any noise I made, so I'd decided to sneak in and lay down a scent trail. Once in the woods, I doused everything with Scent Shield and made some scent drags. On one boot, I used Dominant Buck Lure; on the other, Doe in Heat scent.

Moving slowly, I created a mock deer trail to my stand and beyond, about 500 yards long. Twenty yards out from the stand, I circled several times before I walked down the shooting lane and entered my stand. Removing the scent drags, I placed them in plastic bags inside my fanny pack. I then took out four 35mm scent canisters, placed them about eight feet apart in the shooting lane and covered them with leaves.

There was a very specific method to this madness. My goal was to create confusion and buy myself some time. The scent trail came straight to the tree and then circled. As deer neared the scent canisters, they'd be hit with odors coming from different places, which their innate curiosity would (I hoped) force them to investigate. While the buck's attention was focused down and away from me, I'd have time to get a good shot.

I climbed into the stand, put on warmer boots and settled in. Light soon began to penetrate the gloomy darkness. While scanning the distant shadows about 7:15 a.m., I spotted a deer following the mock trail. Then, there were four more, farther out. They were all does. It didn't take long before all five passed under the tree and into the shooting lane, searching diligently for the deer they could smell but not see. I was really getting a charge out of watching them trying to unravel the puzzle I'd created. It felt great to be so well concealed that the does, just 12 feet away, couldn't detect me.

Then, directly behind my tree, I heard a buck grunt. I froze as the does, startled, looked past me and toward the sound. All at once, I felt a strange mix of fear and excitement. Now I was in a mess. I knew the buck couldn't see me through the thick pine, but now, I had five sets of eyes focused in my direction. Suddenly, I hated does.

What a big dummy I'd been! I don't know how many times the "old guys" had told me to quit watching does and look instead for the buck that was sure to follow. Why hadn't I remembered? In a few seconds, the does turned their attention back to the scent canisters and I could breathe again.

Scent canisters are an easy way to distribute and conserve deer scents. Take several cotton balls, wet them with 10 to 15 drops of scent, drop them into plastic 35mm film canisters and put the lids on. When you get to your stand, take off the lid, place them in a spot where you have an open shooting lane and let the wind bring the deer to you. When you're done hunting, put the lid back on and it will be ready for the next trip. It doesn't hurt to freshen them up by adding more drops each time you go hunting.

Ever so slowly, I pivoted my head to peer through the pine. It was him! Directly behind me, walking with his head down and sniffing the mock trail, was my buck. He was approaching on the same path the does had taken. That meant he was going to walk right under ...

Don't even think now. Stop! My head was pounding, and my chest seemed to tighten. That massive rack was swaying from side to side with each step. It seemed like the whole tree was quivering from my excitement. Get a grip. You must get ready! The does were all looking away, so I stole that moment to stand up, bow in hand, and lean back against the pine. Now I couldn't see him. He was too close, obscured by the limbs. Don't even breathe. He'll hear you.

The does were losing interest and slowly moving away. Looking down between my feet, I watched that gigantic rack suddenly materialize, not 10 feet away. His head was moving back and forth, searching for danger. I was so close I could see that massive chest rising and falling and could hear the sound of his nostrils taking the scent. Nothing I'd ever experienced had prepared me for the intensity of that moment.

Cautiously, one step at a time, he moved toward the scent canisters. I couldn't shoot yet. I had to wait for him to move about 20 yards past the base of the tree. There would be nothing in the path of my shot this time.

The author abandoned deer hunting after his grandfather passed away, but he eventually returned to the sport. The result was one of the most magnificent whitetails in Ohio history. Photo courtesy of Bob Haney.

After what seemed like years of waiting, instinct and practice habits took over. The very moment he came into the open and put his head down, I was at full draw. In an instant, I picked the spot and released. There was no thought process at all.

I watched the arrow strike through the back, angling forward into the chest cavity. He bolted away instantly, showing no sign of a hit, and sent the does into flight. The last thing I saw were the bright orange veins protruding from his back. Quite suddenly, I was gripped by fear. If there was no exit wound, I realized, there may be no blood trail. My first impulse was to jump out of the tree and run after him, but I forced myself to stay put. The wind kicked up, and again, a light rain began to fall.

Have faith, I told myself. The shot was good. But, is there a blood trail? Would the rain wash it away? Would I even find him?

After 20 minutes, I had to move. There was no blood at the spot of the hit, so I went to the last big tree I saw him pass, about 50 yards away. There were tracks, but still no blood. A sick, sinking feeling seemed to grab the pit of my stomach. Go back! Think! I knew from past trailing jobs what I needed to do, but my mind wasn't working very well. I had to make myself remember what I had been taught and focus only on that.

I went back, figured out his exit route and began looking. Moving slowly, I dropped to my hands and knees and searched every leaf and twig. I found a few tiny blood specks and marked them with an arrow. Circling, I found a few more. As I moved along, I discovered more blood, in heavier concentrations. My heart was still racing.

I actually crawled to within 20 yards of the buck before I saw that awesome rack. It was astounding! I approached slowly, with an arrow nocked, just in case. It wasn't necessary; the monster buck was down for good. I gazed silently, still in awe of his remarkable rack. I had never seen anything like it. I reached down to touch each long tine and wondered why nature had chosen him to be so different. I felt a touch of pride, and also of remorse.

After field-dressing him and dragging him home, I raced off to the deer-check station to register him. Because his rack stuck up higher than the sides of my pickup, he quickly became the center of attention in the small town.

Later, Butch Todd of Cambridge, Ohio, officially scored the buck for Pope & Young and Ohio Big Bucks Club. When all the numbers were tallied, he turned in a net score of 196 5/8 non-typical, or 180 1/8 net typical. His extremely long main beams of 29 4/8 and 30 1/8 inches — plus back tines of 15 2/8 and 15 5/8 inches — helped make him one of the most awesome basic 8-pointers ever taken!

I am still extremely proud to have matched wits with a world- class whitetail and won, but I certainly don't deserve all the credit. I was blessed to have received the teachings of serious deer hunters, men who believed in the hunting tradition and who recognized the importance of passing it from generation to generation. I also am lucky enough to have a supportive wife who helps me pursue my dreams. But, I'm still trying to learn, still trying to get better. After all, before long, I'll be one of the "old guys" myself.

Chapter Five

The Third-Wish Trophy

by Steve Vaughn

Wishes, as we all know, don't always come true. But every once in awhile they do — even if the wish is as difficult to attain as a Boone & Crockett whitetail. All it takes, I've learned, is a couple decades of effort, the right location and, maybe, a mysterious prophecy from your wife. In fact, if you're lucky, you might even fulfill three wishes at the same time.

First, of course, you need something to wish for. When I was a boy, my desire was simple: I just wanted to go deer hunting. Even though deer were scarce in Georgia those days, I had dreamed about hunting whitetails for as long as I could remember. But because my dad didn't hunt and nobody else I knew needed a hunting companion with my experience(or lack thereof), I had to wait. Finally, when I reached the magical age of 16, I was issued a driver's license from the State of Georgia. With that license, I could take myself deer hunting. It was all I wanted.

Back then, I wasn't concerned with killing a buck. That would have been great, of course, but it was far more than I dared hope for. No, my goal was just to go hunting. Looking back, I realize how important it is to know what you really want from a hunt. The plans you make, the actions you take and the satisfaction you derive from any hunt all depend upon your goals and expectations.

That first hunt was everything I dreamed it would be. I didn't kill a buck, but I did see my first flash of a white tail from an escaping deer. My

With time running out on his South Texas hunt, the author fulfilled a long-time goal when he took this majestic Boone & Crockett whitetail. Netting 174 3/8 points from a gross score of 186 5/8, the wide-racked buck featured 14 points and main beams that exceeded 28 inches in length. Photo by David Morris.

big moment came when I helped another hunter carry his five-pointer back to camp. It was the first real buck I had ever seen, and there I was actually touching this incredible animal. As we carried the buck, blood dripped onto the leg of my hunting pants. Those stained trousers became my most prized possession, never to see the inside of my mother's washing machine. My status changed that day, at least in my eyes. I had been deer hunting. I was a veteran. I had become a real deer hunter. And, another important change was also occurring. What I now wanted most was to take my first buck.

It took four more years of hunting to get that buck. Again, deer were somewhat rare in Georgia, and hunting success didn't come easily. But, the time and effort involved made the experience all the more rewarding, and it taught me much about hunting deer.

As the years passed, other changes occurred in my life that helped shape my deer hunting goals. My intense fascination with hunting and fishing led me to create an outdoor publishing business by the name of

Game & Fish Publications, Inc. Among the many magazines it publishes is *North American WHITETAIL*, whose first issue appeared in 1982. *WHITETAIL* reflected a new respect for what was rapidly becoming America's No. 1 big game animal. We filled its pages with the most outstanding specimens we could locate throughout the continent. At the same time, we focused on the biological needs and game management techniques so critical to the future prosperity of this great species. And last, but certainly not least, we presented the most advanced hunting tactics available to the serious trophy deer hunter.

Knowing what you really want from a deer hunting experience is critical. If you decide that what you most want is to relax and just enjoy being outdoors, then that's what you should do. If you have a more specific goal, then commit yourself to that purpose and do everything you can to attain it.

The success of *WHITETAIL* brought many changes to deer hunting in America, and as its publisher, I also changed into a trophy hunter. What I grew to want most of all was a Boone & Crockett buck.

Without doubt, a B&C whitetail is one of the rarest and most magnificent of all game trophies. As with beauty, of course, a trophy buck is in the eye of the beholder. What represents the trophy rack of a lifetime to one hunter might be just another set of horns to someone else. But, the elaborate system of steel tapes and independent judges used to score B&C heads serves as an objective standard for measuring the ultimate trophy — a "book" deer. To set out to claim such a trophy was going to be a challenge indeed.

In 1987, I was lucky enough to be invited to hunt a large private ranch in the Brush Country of South Texas. This area of the state is well known for its large bucks and has produced more than its share of Boone & Crocketts over the years. For the past two seasons, my partners in *North American WHITETAIL*, David Morris and Chuck Larsen, along with our friend, Richard Jackson, had hunted trophy bucks on this 100,000-acre Webb County ranch. Managed intensively for deer and other wildlife, the ranch serves as a site for some of the most progressive wildlife research projects in the country.

Our friend and host, Bob Zaiglin, is head of wildlife operations for the ranch. Bob suggested that we bring our wives that year to hunt for what are commonly called "management bucks." It didn't take long for my wife, Louisa, to accept.

The rules were simple — ladies came first. For the first two days of our eight-day hunt, the women could shoot any mature buck with eight points or less. Removing such bucks upgrades the herd, thus they are called "management bucks." The husbands could help the women in their quests but could not hunt during these two days. We would be doing some scouting while also lending a helping hand to our wives.

Successful hunters are often asked to explain the "secret" of taking trophy whitetails. The answer is actually quite simple. If you want to kill big bucks, make sure you're hunting in a place where there are big bucks. If you're not, all the hunting secrets in the world won't help you achieve your goal.

Louisa was excited about the prospects of the hunt. She has hunted with me many times and truly enjoys it. Although her biggest buck at the time was an impressive 12-pointer, she knew this ranch was home to some super 8-pointers with width, mass and tine length that could dwarf any deer she had ever killed. Her strategy was to resist taking one of the many good "eights" that could be seen in an average day's hunt and hold out for the best deer of her life. She knew it would take luck, but she said she felt lucky.

In the darkness of that first morning, we were reunited with a good friend from past hunts, Lane Sumner, a biologist who serves as a guide on the ranch. Don Whitaker, a Texas Tech graduate student who was working on a new deer-study project, also joined our hunting party. Before concentrating our efforts in a single area of the huge ranch, we decided to "high-rack" our way through the property that first morning to get a better idea of what the deer were doing. A common practice on South Texas ranches, high-racking involves riding in an elevated stand mounted on the bed of a pickup. This enables you to get a good view while covering a lot of real estate. Don drove, and Lane joined Louisa and me in the high rack.

The morning broke warm and overcast, but we saw several nice bucks, including one wide, heavy 8-pointer that tested Louisa's resolve to hold out for the big one. After several moments of "should I or shouldn't I," she relaxed the grip on her .270. She said she was still feeling lucky and wanted to continue the search for something better.

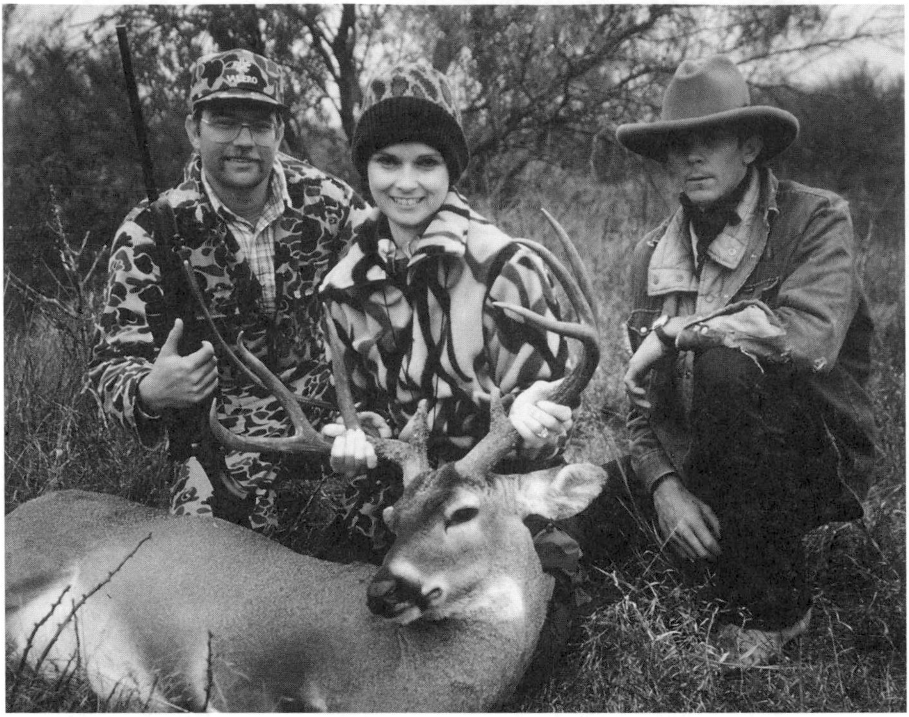

With eight points, long beams and a 22-inch spread, this handsome whitetail was truly a last minute trophy for Louisa Vaughn. It also marked the fulfillment of her "second wish." Lane Sumner (left) and Don Whitaker (right) assisted on the December hunt. Photo by Steve Vaughn.

By mid-morning, the South Texas sun had burned through the morning overcast and the heat was beginning to build. As deer movement slowed, the intensity of our early morning hunting gave way to some relaxed conversation about the ranch. Lane told us that the big news recently was a remarkable sighting of a lone bull buffalo several weeks earlier by a ranch employee. No one knew where, how or why a buffalo would just appear out of nowhere in South Texas, but the guy stuck by his story and had shown the tracks to several ranch biologists. Louisa and I agreed that was a bizarre event, even for Texas. "I really wish we could see that buffalo," she said casually.

The conversation then drifted to another topic as we drove on. A minute later, in the middle of 100,000 acres of Texas brush country, Don's foot slammed down on the brake pedal. There, some 50 yards in front of our pickup, stood 2,000 pounds of brown-maned, bull-chested buffalo. For the next 10 seconds no one spoke and no one moved a muscle as we stared in disbelief. Then, the buffalo, obviously having seen enough, stepped into the thick mesquite and vanished.

I looked at Lane, Lane looked at me and then we both looked at Louisa. She was standing there, obviously pleased with herself, with that smug "I told you so" look on her face. "I told you I felt lucky," she said. "I wished for us to see that buffalo, and there he was."

This was one of those baffling situations that makes you stop and think. The logical side of your brain rationalizes that it was a mere coincidence the buffalo appeared when it did. But, the other side of the brain says, "Wait a second, man. She may be on to something, so you better not argue."

It was Lane who spoke first. "You must be right about that lucky feeling," he told Louisa. "But wishes come in threes, and you've got two left."

We quickly reached a tongue-in-cheek agreement that Louisa would carefully save her remaining two wishes until we needed them to guarantee the success of the hunt.

On the second and last day of Louisa's hunt, the women only had until 1 p.m. to get their deer. At that time, they would have to meet back at ranch headquarters in order to drive to San Antonio for their plane trip home. The deer were holding tight to the thick brush that morning, and as time wound down, last-day pressures began to mount. I was seated on the right side of the high rack, peering intently into every gap in the brush as we slowly eased along a seldom-used ranch road. But, there was nothing to see.

About noon, I felt Lane make a sudden movement as if he had spotted a deer. As I whirled in his direction, he intentionally placed his hand in front of my face to block my view. All I could see was a glimpse of a white flag as it disappeared into the brush to the left. One look at his face told me what had happened. "I couldn't let you see that buck," he told me. "If you saw what I just saw, I'm not sure you could follow the rules and not shoot today!"

His face was still pale as he described an enormously wide buck with main beams the size of a man's wrist and a rack that he believed held at least 12 points. He had seen the buck for just a moment as it was running away, but he'd seen enough to realize we'd have to return here. We carefully noted the location.

It was now past noon, the sun high and bright and the day unusually hot for mid-December. The deer weren't moving and there was less than an hour to hunt. The CB radio in the cab of the pickup crackled, and Don brought us to a halt. Chuck Larsen and his wife, Jean, were calling from another part of the ranch. They had come across two bucks that had locked antlers while fighting. It was one of those rare sights that merited some photography. The problem was that the camera equipment was in our truck. We'd have to go, and travel fast, to get there. In all probability, it meant the end of Louisa's hunt.

Louisa was unperturbed. "Don't give up quite yet," she said calmly. "I think I'll use my second wish and wish for my buck to show up."

Lane and I nodded in agreement, saying nothing, but we knew full well that we couldn't possibly cover the distance to Chuck and Jean in the short time we had left and still have any hope of hunting at the same time.

Sixty seconds later, with our truck churning up the dust on a bumpy ranch road, Don's foot slammed the brake pedal as Lane yanked the signal rope. Fifty yards away, bedded down in the shade of a pear cactus, was an 8-point buck with a 22-inch inside spread, 5-inch bases, long main beams and exceptional tine length.

This time, Louisa never hesitated. The shot rang out from her .270, and in minutes, we were loading her trophy into the truck. The second wish had produced the best buck of her life.

I looked at Lane, Lane looked at me and then we both looked at Louisa. She simply stood there, obviously pleased with herself. We recognized the same "I told you so" expression we'd seen the day before.

We made it to Chuck and Jean in time to photograph the incredible locked bucks and then headed back to headquarters to prepare for the women's departure.

Just as she was about to leave, Louisa took Lane and me aside. "You know, I've got one wish left," she said. I looked at Lane, Lane looked at me and then we both looked at Louisa. "For my third wish, I wish that you will get your Boone & Crockett buck!"

That night, after filling ourselves with a South Texas ranch supper, Lane and I began our hunting plans. We had six days to concentrate on 100,000 acres of some of the best hunting country in existence. Although we had seen several good bucks during Louisa's hunt, Lane was most interested in the buck he had shielded from my view earlier in the day. He

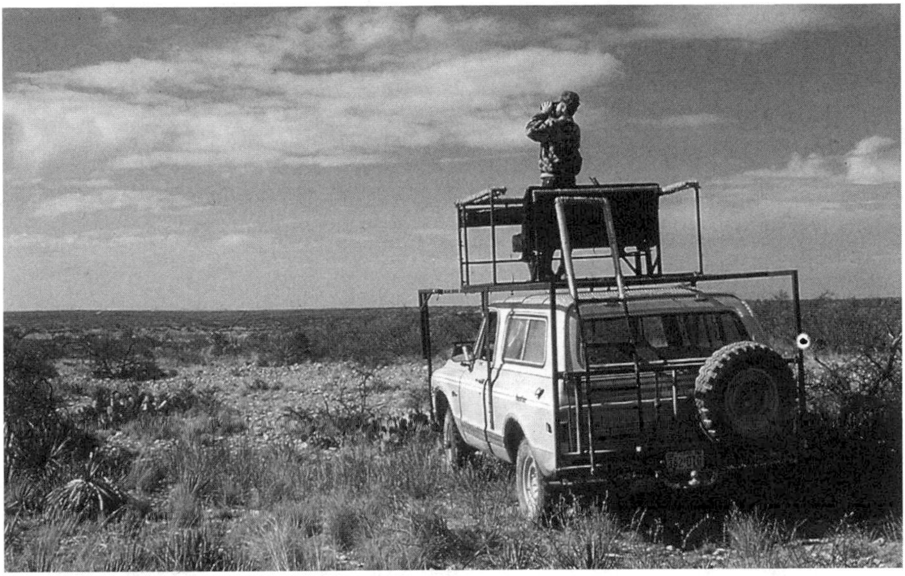

High racks like this one provide South Texas hunters with the elevation they need to see over vast stretches of mesquite and brush. The author's novel use of a high rack helped him outwit an elusive Boone & Crockett whitetail at the last minute. Photo by Gordon Whittington.

wanted a better look and so did I. We quickly agreed to head back there during the peak movement period at first light.

We left the bunkhouse well before dawn. Though the weather was unseasonably warm, I still felt confident. We were in the area by the time we had good shooting light, and the does were moving. Two were feeding in almost the exact spot where the huge buck had been the day before. Anticipation was high, but no buck appeared. After an hour or so, we moved on to other areas.

The next day, Lane wanted to try a section of the ranch which we had not yet hunted. Before Louisa and I arrived, he had seen several good bucks there and thought it was worth looking over. Since it was early in our hunt and it's always interesting to try new country, I agreed.

We spent all day and half of the next hunting that part of the ranch. Lane had been right — we saw several trophy bucks, including one 10-pointer with an inside spread I estimated at 23 inches. Big bucks have a bad habit of never giving you enough time to study them, but this buck did just the opposite. I spotted him through an opening in thick brush, and because he thought he was hidden, he stayed put. At 50 yards, my binoculars brought home every detail of his wide trophy rack. This close examination probably saved his life. I judged him to be in the mid-160s, about five inches short of the record-book proportions I was seeking. We continued to hunt, in the back of my mind, counting on Louisa's third wish.

It's easier to pass up bucks if you've given careful thought, in advance, to exactly how high your standards will be on the hunt. Make sure, however, that you don't set your standards higher than what is possible for that particular area. Know what the realistic top-end potential is and set your target accordingly.

In the heat of that third afternoon, I pressed Lane to tell me more about the huge buck he glimpsed during Louisa's hunt. He repeated his description of enormously wide main beams and at least 12 points. "I think you'd shoot him," he added.

We had just enough time to make it back to that area, and I decided to give it a shot. We arrived late in the day, catching the peak movement period just before dark. Again, we saw does but no buck.

That night, I had to make a decision. Half of the six days were gone, and it was time to consider my strategy. I usually like to use the first half of a hunt to look things over, determine what's going on and figure out where the best potential exists. In the second half of a hunt, I focus on that best area so I can maximize my chances for success. Lane had glimpsed the best buck we'd seen so far, and even though I had not seen its rack, I trusted Lane's judgment. The problem was, we hadn't seen the buck since the second day of Louisa's hunt.

I played back the events of the last few days in my mind. We had encountered the huge buck late in the morning. We had returned the next morning during the peak movement period at dawn. This afternoon, we had hunted through the prime period just before dark. This mental review instantly isolated a potential problem. We had not checked on the buck during the same late-morning time period during which he first had been spotted. I decided to focus on that huge buck and hunt him late the next morning.

At dawn, I went over my thoughts with Lane, and we laid out a hunting plan that would put us back in the buck's area close to the same time we had seen him earlier. The morning passed slowly until it was time to approach the buck's area. When we did, I saw him instantly.

He stood 200 yards away, staring right at me. Lane and I froze, but it was too late. The buck turned and simply melted into the mesquite. It all happened in just a few seconds, but at least now, I had finally seen the buck. I heard Lane whisper, "That was him. Did you see him?"

I tried to mentally reconstruct the image of the buck. He had been standing, slightly silhouetted against the late-morning sky, not more than 10 yards from spot where Lane had seen him five days earlier. My straight-ahead view confirmed a width of at least 25 inches, with very heavy mass. As the huge buck had turned and entered the brush, it seemed that tines were everywhere. The image was too confusing to count points, but I knew he had plenty of them. "Yes," I whispered back to Lane. "We've found our buck."

Being able to find the specific buck you want and then hunting him leads to one of the greatest thrills a trophy hunter can enjoy. Whether it's an actual sighting or the discovery of the buck's sign, nothing creates more anticipation and drama than going one-on-one with a particular deer. It's the ultimate deer hunting challenge.

Quietly, we left in the same direction we had come, not wanting to further disturb the buck. We needed time to plan our next move.

A great many things had occurred in the span of a few short seconds. We had found the buck I wanted to kill, but more importantly, much could be learned now about where he was and what he was doing. Success or failure depended upon making the right judgments.

The buck had been in the same place both times we saw him, and he had been there during the same hour of the day. Each time he was spotted, he moved quickly into the brush, but appeared to go only a short distance. The area was part of a gently sloping hillside that extended northeast and was somewhat sheltered from the hot afternoon sun. The brush consisted of clumps of mesquite that were just close enough together to provide good cover yet still allow for breezes to penetrate them. A windmill less than a quarter-mile away provided water.

Everything added up to this being the buck's midday bedding area. It also explained why we never saw him during our two attempts at dawn and dusk. The deer were late in the pre-rut period, but the warm, dry weather was holding back the onset of full rut. Our buck was probably active in the cooler temperatures of early morning and late evening, but

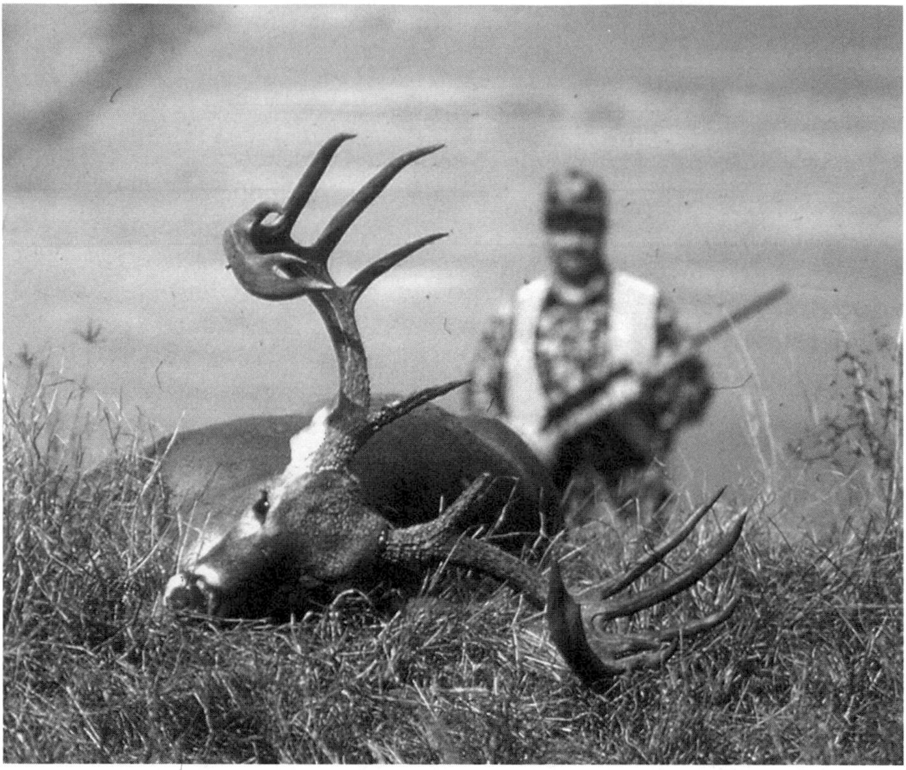

Almost every deer hunter dreams of walking up on a trophy buck like this one. The author's wish came true when he claimed this record-book whitetail in Texas. Photo by David Morris.

he was spending the warmer hours in his bedding area.

The weather forecast for the next few days called for more of the same. That was good, because I didn't want a sudden cold snap to trigger the rut and cause the buck to change his routine. Now, all I had to do was figure out a way to hunt this buck without spooking him. If I made just one mistake, I'd never have enough time to relocate him on 100,000 acres.

Few hunting challenges are as difficult as killing a buck while he's in his chosen bedding area. After all, security is the main reason he chose it. The best plan is to get him in the morning when he's returning to that bedding area. I knew our next move would come in the morning, but I needed the right tactic.

There are really only two basic tactics for a deer hunter to select. You can go to the deer, or you can let the deer come to you. If you go to the deer, the odds are greatly in its favor. That's because if you don't get him, you will almost assuredly spook him away from the area.

I decided to try option No. 2 and let this buck come to me. I knew the deer were responding well to rattling, as they usually do when it's this close to the rut in South Texas. I also figured our buck would be returning to his bedding area in the morning following a night on the town. Lane and I could move in at dawn and set up in a good ambush location. Lane would rattle while I waited 30 or 40 yards downwind to welcome our heavy-horned visitor. We would stay far enough away from the buck's actual bedding area to avoid violating his security, yet we'd be close enough for the sound of Lane's rattling horns to reach his ears. I felt good about the plan.

The more you can learn about the location, routines and tendencies of a buck, the better your odds for success. Uncovering this knowledge and being able to formulate a strategy with that information are the skills by which great trophy hunters are measured.

As dawn broke on the morning of day five, Lane and I were in position in what felt like a perfect setup. Rattling creates its own drama and excitement, and as Lane began working the horns, every muscle in my body tightened. Four hours later, however, they had relaxed considerably. The buck never showed. Sometimes, you never know why a plan didn't work; it's just an unsettling feeling that deer hunters learn to live with. Lane and I quietly slipped away, retreating back along the path that had brought us there.

Don was waiting with the pickup truck at our prearranged meeting place. He handed us each a Coke and listened politely as we vented our frustrations. Complaining can be helpful at times, but it's never killed a deer. Soon, we were back to planning, trying to figure out the best way to utilize what little time I had left to hunt.

If the buck wasn't going to come to us, I knew we would have to become more aggressive in going to him. A stalk into his bedding area was out of the question. Visibility would be poor in the 10-foot-high mesquite, and the dry grass and twigs would announce every footstep. Some elevation would improve visibility considerably, but to use a treestand in South Texas, you have to bring your own tree. What they do use there are long-legged tripods, but they're noisy and difficult to set up quickly. Besides, I had no reason to believe this buck was blind or stupid. The unfamiliar sight of a tripod and hunter towering above the mesquite near his bedding area would hardly go unnoticed.

I voiced this problem out loud, and Don came to my rescue. "He is familiar with the ranch trucks," he noted. "The road you first saw him from runs right by his bedding area."

That could work! We'd get the pickup with the tallest high rack, which would provide plenty of elevation. Plus, the boxed-in bench on top would provide cover for us. If we started right away, we could park it on the ranch road next to his bedding area and then drive away in the other truck. Our buck would have the rest of the day and all night to get used to the truck sitting on the road. Before dawn the next morning, Lane and I would sneak up the dirt road, climb into the parked high rack and wait for the huge buck to return to his bedding area. We had our plan.

The more your buck knows about what you're doing, the better the odds that he, not you, will be the successful one. In the formulation of every plan, you must consider what it will teach the deer you are hunting and how he will react.

The next morning found Lane and me sitting motionless in the high rack, overlooking the same location where we had first seen the buck with Louisa. It was warm and overcast, just as it had been for the last six days. All was quiet the first 30 minutes. Then, two does entered the area, fed calmly and disappeared. By 10 a.m., the sun had climbed above us and the temperature began to rise.

Suddenly, not 50 yards from where we sat, the sound of antlers rubbing against brush caused my adrenaline to surge. Slowly, I raised my gun and rested it on the wall of the high-rack. I had to be ready if the buck appeared from the thick brush. The seconds dragged into minutes, and the minutes felt like hours. Then, 175 yards out, I saw him. He had an enormously wide rack, with main beams the size of a man's wrist and what looked to be at least 12 points. He stepped into an opening in the mesquite.

After six long days of hunting, this was the chance I'd been waiting for ever since Louisa had departed. The shot rang out and I relaxed my grip on my 7mm magnum. Another buck now required loading into the truck.

The third wish had produced the best buck of my life.

Six months later, the postman delivered an envelope from the

Boone & Crockett Club. As I opened it, Louisa watched. Inside was my official certificate documenting the final net typical score of 174 3/8, easily surpassing the 170 minimum required to make the book. The tapes and the judges had recorded the buck as a 14-pointer with an outside spread of 26 inches and main beams of 28 inches. All four circumferences exceeded four inches, and the total gross score, before deductions, was 186 5/8.

I looked up at Louisa. She stood there, obviously pleased with herself, and gave me that now-familiar look. "I told you so," she said.

Chapter Six

Magic And Madness In The Montana Mountains

by David Morris

In a lifetime of deer hunting, I've come to expect the unexpected.

Take my 1993 season, for example. Traveling to Alberta for a hunt, I came oh-so-close to shooting three different trophy bucks but somehow went home empty-handed. When I headed to northern Saskatchewan, a tough, bone-chilling hunt was looking bad until a 160-class 9-pointer changed everything by wandering beneath my tree stand on the fourth day. And later in South Texas, I spent almost a week chasing a single buck before I finally pulled the plug at the last minute and decided to completely change my tactics, locations, strategy and target. Just as time was winding down, I was rewarded with a beautiful 170-class 10-pointer.

But none of my hunts that year — or any other year, for that matter — could have prepared me for the week my friends and I spent chasing whitetails near my home in northwestern Montana. For my three visitors from Georgia — Melvin, Stevie and Ed — this was a much-anticipated hunt. So when we met at my hunting cabin in the hills west of Kalispell, I decided to do everything I could to help them get their bucks. As it turned out, I had no idea exactly what that would entail.

What follows is the day-to-day account, as recorded in my diary, of

The author took this fine Montana 10-pointer after locating running deer tracks in fresh snow and following them to a breeding party. Photo by Jennifer Morris.

that memorable hunt — a week, I might add, which marked the end of what loosely could be referred to as my "guiding career."

Thursday, November 18

6 a.m. — After my two Canadian trips, it's good to be back to the "warmer" climes of Montana — except that it's too warm for deer hunting. Highs are in the 50s and there's no snow. The deer aren't going to be moving much in this weather, but today is the traditional start of the Montana rut. That'll help. We're going to scatter out this morning, look around and try to get a handle on what's going on.

12 noon — It's quiet out there. Too quiet. I checked a cutover that was hot last year and saw four does and two young bucks at first light. After that, nothing. The deer are bedding down early in this warm weather. About 10 o'clock this morning, smoke from burning slash piles led me to a recently completed logging operation. I found good sign there, includ-

Montana hunters Len Patterson (left) and Derek Schulz shot these two Boone and Crockett bucks on the last day of the 1992 season, both within a couple miles of the author's hunting cabin. Len's buck scored 188 5/8 and Derek's 173. Enduring sub-zero temperatures is worth it for a chance at great bucks like these. Photo by David Morris.

ing some promising buck rubs. Deer here really flock to fresh cutovers, because they like to eat the moss on the downed trees. I'm going to look for some other logging operations right after lunch, and unless something better turns up, I'll end up back where they're burning.

7:15 p.m. — I found two more recent logging areas with encouraging sign. Neither were better than the cutover I found this morning, though, so that's where I spent the last two hours. Does and fawns started showing up right away. About 30 minutes before dark, a 130-class 8-pointer ambled in. He was more interested in eating than in the half dozen does around him. I even did some rattling within sight of him, and he hardly looked my way. There's not much evidence of the rut. At last light, a good buck moved through at the edge of my vision, but I couldn't tell exactly what he was. The other guys haven't seen much, except a wolf in the yard of the cabin. Interesting place, this Montana.

Friday, November 19

6:45 a.m. — If the weather report is correct, we've got a humdinger of a cold front moving in here tomorrow night. They're talking about up to a foot of snow and temperatures below zero. I'll believe it when I see it. It's plain muggy out there now. I hope they're right, though. That's exactly what we need to get these deer on the move and kick off the rut.

Areas with fresh timber harvests can be deer magnets, especially in northern big-woods settings where there are few other competing food sources. Heavy snow only increases the appeal of these areas. The best spots have enough cover remaining in them to provide deer with a sense of security and safety.

After looking around yesterday, it's become obvious the bucks are bedding above the cutovers and coming down to feed. Hunting low is okay in the afternoon, but the best plan for morning hunts would be to get above the cutover and intercept the bucks as they return to bed. That's exactly what Ed and I are going to do this morning.

12:10 p.m. — We had some excitement but didn't quite connect. Not knowing the lay of the land very well, it was 8:45 before we found a good setup, which turned out to be a bald knob overlooking the high side of the cutover. Dense lodgepole pines, which make perfect bedding cover, stretched far up the hill behind us. We had just settled in when deer started filtering by.

Even when the time is right for the rut, unusually warm weather will suppress the ritual rutting activity that we hunters depend upon. Cold fronts, on the other hand, will normally trigger rutting activity. However, if the temperature falls too far below what is normal for that region, rutting may not pick up until temperatures begin to moderate.

The first one was a spike. Soon after came a yearling 6-pointer. Next, a couple of does meandered by. At 9:20, a doe ran through an opening about 150 yards below us. I had my binoculars locked on the opening when a 140-class 8-pointer hurried across seconds later. If they stayed their course, their route would take them up a fairly open draw about 100 yards to the left. That's were I had Ed train his .308. Unfortunately, we had seen the last of that buck. I have no idea where he went. I tried rattling him in but managed only a forkhorn, our last deer of the morning. Stevie has to return to Georgia tomorrow so I'm hunting with him this afternoon.

8:40 p.m. — Frustration. We had him . . . almost. Stevie and I started the afternoon looking for some new areas and checking the other cutovers I'd found earlier. We didn't find anything we liked better than that first place, so we headed there at 3:30. About 300 yards into the cutover, a very good buck walked nonchalantly across the trail 75 yards in front of us, right at a logger's loading deck. With any luck, I figured we could catch him standing in the bald open. We eased slowly forward, Stevie with his rifle at ready and me with my 10X binoculars poised for duty. I was delighted by the prospects of pulling a last-minute trophy out of the hat for Stevie.

There are two keys to finding deer quickly through a scope. First, if you're using a variable scope, set the power reasonably low, such as 3X or 4X, especially in tight cover. This allows you to see a wider field of view. Secondly, and perhaps most importantly, keep both eyes open and concentrate on the deer as you raise the rifle. It's just like instinctively pointing your finger at a distant object, only the rifle barrel substitutes for your finger. Never close one eye and try to locate the deer by moving the rifle around. The off-eye should be closed only after the deer is in your sights.

When we reached the edge of the loading dock, we inched forward and peeked around the last bit of brush. The buck was there, 60 yards away on the far side of the opening. Binoculars weren't necessary to see he was a shooter. Before I even raised my glasses, I issued the go-ahead to Stevie, who was slightly behind me and to my right. The buck was quite a sight through 10-power magnification. Quartering away, his thick neck bulged as he looked back at us with growing concern. His rack was very tall but not that wide, maybe 18 inches. On the strength of those 10 long points, he'd score better than 150.

As I studied the buck, it dawned on me that Stevie should have already fired. "Shoot him, Stevie," I whispered. Precious seconds passed. "Shoot him, Stevie!" I said again, with mounting urgency. Then came a response, but not the one I was expecting.

"I can't find him in the scope!"

I snapped my head around to find Stevie wiggling the rifle barrel in small circles, his left eye tightly shut. "Open both eyes," I instructed, "look at the deer and then point the rifle at him." Stevie did so and immediately

Because of the light hunting pressure, northwestern Montana has plenty of older bucks and a tight buck/doe ratio, making rattling an effective tool for hunters in and around the rut. This fine buck responded to the author's rattling early in the 1993 season. Photo by David Morris.

said he could see the buck . . . just as it bounded off. I'm not sure which of us was more disappointed.

Saturday, November 20

6:15 a.m. — Something's astir with this weather. It's warm and ominously overcast — like the calm before the storm. The weather forecast is still calling for a major change tonight, and they could be right. Stevie's gone home. Too bad he didn't get his buck.

Melvin, Ed and I are going to hunt a remote basin this morning where I saw several good bucks last year. I've held off hunting there until deer activity picked up because it requires a two-mile hike over a steep ridge to reach it. But if it snows as much as predicted, we might not be able to get there later. Besides, with a front of this magnitude coming in, the deer may be moving in advance of it. Ed's going to accompany me this morning. Melvin will parallel us by a couple hundred yards.

2:45 p.m. — We're some tired troopers. We must have walked 10 miles this morning, seemingly all uphill. But things are heating up in deerdom.

We were late getting to the basin because we got hung up in a herd of about 20 mule deer as we topped the ridge. We got to where I wanted to hunt about 9 o'clock, and Ed and I quickly rattled in a young 8-pointer and a second unidentified buck. A couple more rattling sequences yielded nothing.

We then began slipping through a huge area of open timber that had been thinned two years earlier. This is a favorite feeding area and is seldom disturbed because of its remoteness. As a result, deer frequent this area during all hours of the day. Patches of thick cover scattered throughout the open timber offer just enough concealment to attract big bucks. Ed and I had just rounded a bend on a logging road in one of those thick patches when a dandy buck appeared 30 yards in front of us. He didn't wait around. I regretted blundering into him, but I was encouraged to spot a mature buck on his feet; it's something we haven't seen much of the last two days.

An hour and a handful of does later, we walked up on a buck standing watch over a doe some 100 yards away on a sidehill. Ed wanted something scoring at least 140, and a quick check with the binoculars told me the 10-pointer just made the grade. I gave Ed the thumbs-up at the same time the two deer, which had also seen us, started up the hill. But by expertly utilizing every shred of cover, the two whitetails were able to slip away, denying Ed a clean shot. Truthfully, though, I had mixed emotions about that buck getting away. After all, the nearest road was two miles away over a not-insignificant hill, and Ed still had several days of hunting left.

We saw only one more buck, a 125-class 10-pointer hot after a doe, as we topped the hill en route to the truck about 2 o'clock. Elk sign was everywhere on the ridge, something I need to remember next October.

9:00 p.m. — The predicted storm is upon us. The wind is blowing, the snow is falling and the temperature's dropping faster than the '29 stock market. It's already in the high teens. Rutting activity can't be far behind.

This afternoon, I went alone and hunted an isolated, timbered hill surrounded by a big area of various-aged clearcuts. On the way up the hill,

I spied a 140-class 8-pointer lying with a doe. I watched the pair for several minutes from 40 yards away, wishing that Melvin or Ed were with me. The two deer finally got tired of the audience, stood up, stretched and walked off.

My destination was a high saddle I had found the previous spring while looking for sheds. A small pond rests at the top of the saddle, and an alder-lined drainage runs down the hill from the pond. The area had many impressive rubs last spring. One of the hills forming the saddle is open on top and makes a perfect ambush point. With daylight running out, I was in a hurry to reach the hill and my haste may well have cost me a huge buck. Just as I was breaking out of the cover next to the open hillside, I noticed movement at the very spot where I had intended to position myself. I looked up to see a buck with a wall of tines trotting leisurely over the hill! I'm still kicking myself for my carelessness.

A breeding party consists of a hot doe, at least one buck and whatever entourage may be accompanying them. Often, more than one buck will be in the chase after the hot doe, and it's not unusual for a couple of other does to join the festivities. Fresh snow during the peak of the rut offers a great opportunity to locate these breeding parties. The telltale sign is two or more sets of running tracks. Breeding parties often circle or mill around the same general area. Plus, because they are absorbed in what they're doing and are far less wary than normal, they are easier to approach.

Sunday, November 21

6:30 a.m. — Talk about cold . . . and snow! Ed just struck a pose for the camera next to the thermometer on the deck. It reads a cool 28 below! Judging from what's on the truck, over a foot of snow fell. I'm really in no hurry to get out there, and not just because it's so bitter. I just don't think the deer will be moving early in this kind of cold and after so much snow. When the sun warms things up later this morning, the deer should start stirring, and I hope they have lovin' on their minds. I also hope the trucks will crank. Ed's out there now trying mightily to open the truck door, which seems to be securely frozen shut.

12:15 p.m. — Thank God for wood stoves. We may not warm up again until next summer, although my blood was running pretty hot about an hour ago! Melvin and I teamed up this morning and returned to where

Generally, mule deer occupy the ridges and whitetails live in the valleys and lower elevations. However, big whitetails frequently are found in the higher elevations right alongside the mule deer, especially early in the season before the lure of the rut draws them down. Photo by David Morris.

I saw the big buck last night. We spotted very little sign there and started looking around for some activity. One of my favorite tricks after a fresh snow during the rut is to cover a lot of country in search of running deer tracks, figuring that those tracks will have been made by a breeding party. When I've found tracks like that in the past, I've had extraordinary luck at trailing up the breeding party or rattling bucks into view when I get near the party. The ideal setting is hilly country with relatively open cover, where the deer can be seen from a distance. Melvin and I were in that kind of place late this morning when we came across running-deer tracks — with the hooves still in them!

When we spotted the tracks, we were coursing a clearcut that had been replanted in widely spaced lodgepole pines, four to five feet tall. After studying the area briefly, I visually traced the likely route of the breeding party up the hill and suddenly found myself staring at two does and a whopper buck standing 150 yards away. The buck was alternately tending one of the does and casting glances back at us. No judging was necessary; this was a shooter. I told Melvin to take him. My binoculars had just settled on the buck when I heard the shot and saw a cloud of snow erupt in front of the deer. "You missed," I yelled. "Shoot again!"

In lunging bounds, the big buck was plowing through the deep snow at a slight quartering angle to us. Melvin touched off another 160-grain Nosler from his 7mm Rem. Mag. and again kicked up snow, this time off the buck's bow. The sound of the striking bullet apparently confused the buck and he stopped momentarily, partially obscured by a small lodgepole. When Melvin fired the third shot, I didn't see where the bullet hit. For the first time, I thought he might have connected. But, that hope dimmed when I saw the speed with which the buck covered the last 25 yards to the top of the ridge. Pale and exhausted-looking, Melvin turned and said, "I had to have hit him!"

He hadn't, as our search soon proved. We followed the bounding buck, which had split off from the does, for a quarter-mile and found no sign of a hit. We returned to camp in considerable despair.

Chances to take big bucks are rare, and a serious trophy hunter must be able to take full advantage of the few opportunities that come along. This means being able to make the shots — not just the easy ones but the hard ones, too. In my opinion, the two major keys to good shooting are trigger control and the use of a rest. They can be mastered only by practice, practice and more practice. Never jerk the trigger, and never take a shot without using a rest to steady the gun if one is available.

I'm not sure exactly how big the buck was, but I did notice he had an unmatched tine on one side, suggesting that he was probably a 9 or an 11-pointer. I'm guessing a nine. Either way, he was big — wide, heavy and tall. If he's an 11-pointer, he's book-class. If he's a nine, he'll score in the 160s. It hurts to miss a chance at a buck like that.

8:20 p.m. — Melvin and I tried it again this afternoon. Getting these guys a good buck is becoming personal now. We checked several clearcuts and cutovers. If we had been moose hunting, we would've had some action, because we saw two cows and a fairly good bull. It was bitter cold. We couldn't stay away from the truck heater longer than an hour at a time.

Once again, fresh running tracks helped us out as we found tracks from two different parties. The first set led us to a 120-class buck chasing a doe high in a clearcut. The second tracks eventually guided us to a stand of timber that was too thick for us to effectively trail the deer. Instead, we rattled at the edge of the thicket and coaxed out a small 8-pointer, possibly a satellite buck from the breeding party. Some rutting activity is definitely going on, but the extreme cold seems to be hampering their movement. We rattled three or four times unsuccessfully. We ended the afternoon in the clearcut where Melvin had shot at the buck this morning, hoping lightning would strike twice. Only a couple of does showed, but I have a strong suspicion they are the same two does we'd seen with the big buck. We'll be there at daybreak and see if the buck has rejoined them.

Monday, November 22

7:15 a.m. — It's 22 below. The trucks barely cranked. Melvin and I are starting late this morning. I don't want to go into the clearcut where Melvin shot at the buck until we have shooting light, or we might blunder around in the dark and spook the deer. I hope Ed sees something good today. He's hunting hard but can't seem to come up with anything.

12:30 p.m. — What a morning! No buck, but it's not from the lack of opportunity. We got to the clearcut just after shooting light and slipped around the corner so we could see the hillside where the buck was yesterday. To my utter astonishment, the very same buck and three does were standing in exactly the same spot as before. Melvin didn't need me to tell him to shoot. He moved a few feet to my right and knelt down for the shot. The buck was standing and staring at us, maybe 125 yards away. I locked my binoculars on him.

The buck was, in fact, a 9-pointer, but what a 9-pointer! He was very heavy and about 24 inches wide (22 inside). His brow tines were a long seven inches, his G-2s were approaching 12 inches and his G-3s were only slightly shorter than that. His wide, square rack guaranteed long main beams. If his left antler had a six-inch G-4 to match the right antler, the buck would have booked. As it was, he was a 165-class 9-pointer! During the six to eight seconds it took me to size up the buck, no shot came from my partner. "Melvin, shoot!" I pleaded.

Back came all too familiar words. "I can't see him!" cried Melvin in obvious desperation. I looked his way and immediately saw the problem. "You're behind a tree," I told him. "Move this way."

Melvin slid over and quickly fired his first shot as the buck started walking toward the does. The whitetail immediately leaped forward and stormed up the hill. The volley commenced. By the time the echo from

Melvin's fourth shot faded away, the buck had disappeared over the ridge. In the immortal words of Yogi Berra, "It was déjà vu all over again."

There was really no need to check for a hit, but we did anyway, with the same results as the day before. I felt profoundly sorry for Melvin. He's a capable hunter, but seeing huge bucks can do strange things to people. I speak from personal experience.

With hardly a word spoken, we got after them again. During the next two hours, we saw only a moose and a couple coyotes. By late morning, the bright sun had warmed the temperature to a "balmy" 10 degrees, and I felt certain some deer were moving. We just had to find them. At 11 o'clock, we returned to one of the fresh cutovers I had found earlier and saw deer before we'd even parked the truck. We had just pulled up to the edge of the cutover when a good buck trotted from right to left in front of us, obviously trailing something. I grabbed my rattling horns, and we hurried about 125 yards to where we'd last seen the buck. There, we set up to rattle.

Buck fever is real, and it has devastating effects on some people. As simple as it seems, the best way to combat this malady is the age-old technique of taking two or three slow, deep breaths. That is, of course, if the hunter can think clearly enough to do it.

Taking no chances on a shooting snafu this time, I positioned Melvin behind a big log that would serve nicely as a rifle rest. I began the rattling sequence, first rubbing brush and lightly tickling the tines together, then shifting to an all-out thrashing of the antlers. I kept this up for about a minute before dropping the antlers to the snow. The wait began.

The first indication of a response to my rattling came when I heard the snap of a limb. But, it didn't come from the direction the buck had gone, and where Melvin was looking. Instead, it came from behind us, toward the truck. I turned my attention that way but didn't say anything to Melvin, not wanting him to give up his shooting rest just yet. A full minute passed before I saw the buck — a wide 10-pointer — walking no more than 10 yards behind my pickup! I grabbed Melvin by the coat and whispered for him to move to another log that would provide a rest for shooting the buck. Then, I told him something I knew he would find hard to believe.

"Mel, there's a good buck behind the pickup. Aim toward the truck and when he walks out, shoot him. And Mel," I added, half in jest, "don't shoot the truck."

He promptly set up on the log and we waited. I could see the tension in Melvin as he squirmed into a better position and clung to the rifle with a white-knuckled grip. Glassing, I caught a glimpse of movement through the truck's windshield. As strange as it seemed, the buck really was right behind the truck. "Be ready, Mel. He's there."

"Are you sure?" Melvin responded, showing the first sign of doubt.

The buck abruptly answered that question by walking out from behind the vehicle. "When I whistle, he'll stop," I told Melvin. "Then, you shoot."

At the sound of the whistle, the buck came to a halt and casually looked around. I knew — or thought I knew — we had him. When the shot shattered the stillness, the buck, instead of falling, simply looked our way. Melvin turned to me with a disbelieving look on his face and blurted, "I couldn't have missed him!"

The buck, figuring things were getting a little weird, started walking briskly away. "Shoot him again!" I yelled.

He fired another shot, the net result of which was to speed the buck on his way. Melvin hung his head in despair, while I felt dazed by the whole series of events. I refused to believe that buck wasn't dead. Telling Melvin to try to cut off the deer, I hurried to the spot where it had been standing when he shot. On the way, I heard Melvin call. I looked back and saw him pointing feverishly in the direction the buck had gone. He was mouthing the words, "There he is."

The use of rattling horns is a key ingredient in what might be termed "aggressive hunting," in which the hunter tries to make something happen that otherwise would not have occurred. Besides calling in an aggressive buck, rattling horns can be used to stop a moving deer, make a hidden deer expose himself, move a partially obscured deer enough to allow a shot, pull a buck out of cover you cannot effectively hunt or even mask a deer-alerting sound that was made by mistake.

"Shoot him!" I yelled, which by now had a very familiar ring to it.

Melvin raised his rifle, then lowered it, ran a few steps and raised and lowered it once more. Then, he took off at a run, the buck obviously having departed. I continued on toward the buck's tracks. Any sign of a hit would have been easy to see in the deep snow, but there was none. I followed the tracks anyway for a couple hundred yards. While I was doing so, I could see Melvin tracking something off to my right. As it turned out, he was on the trail of the other buck he'd seen after we parted, and it was not the buck he had shot at! Apparently, a second buck had answered our rattling. All in all, it was one of the wildest mornings of my hunting career.

8:15 p.m. — Ed and Melvin just put on a fine feed for dinner — a good ending to an eventful day. Melvin and I went out together again this afternoon, after checking his rifle, I might add. Melvin was clearly disappointed to discover that it was right on target. The afternoon, though quiet compared to the morning, was actually fairly productive. We found a new area where a couple of selective timber thinnings had recently concluded. There was a lot of sign in the fresh cuts, and we saw several deer, including some in two chases. A forkhorn and a 120-class 8-pointer were among the participants in the first chase. I just caught a glimpse of a buck in the second one, but he looked good. We're going to check out that area in the morning.

Ed is seeing some deer now but nothing shootable. He's a good hunter, though, and something should turn up. He did see that same wolf again, about a mile from the cabin this time.

Tuesday, November 23

6:45 a.m. — It has warmed up to zero. We've got an inch of new snow, which will be perfect for locating the breeding parties. Melvin and I are heading to where we left off last night. Time is running out for both him and Ed.

11:30 a.m. — We got our buck. More accurately, I got my buck, though I didn't entirely mean to. It happened this way: Melvin and I reached the cutover we wanted to hunt about daybreak. Easing along slowly, we had seen only a couple of does when we came upon two sets of fresh tracks that had all the earmarks of being a buck and a doe. The tracks led downhill to the left, away from the bench we were on. We slipped up to the edge of the bench and peered over. Standing 60 yards away was a doe. She was slightly hunched with her tail stuck straight out, which is the standard posture of a hot doe. I knew the buck was near, and it didn't take long to find him. He came trotting out from behind a blowdown to the left of the doe. I could tell immediately that he was a 10-pointer, probably scoring in the 150s. Once again those familiar words

Jennifer Morris, the author's daughter, poses with the 130-class 8-pointer she took on Thanksgiving Day, following her father's eventful week of hunting. Photo by David Morris.

rang out: "Shoot him, Mel!"

The buck had picked up his doe and was quickly escorting her to a quieter honeymoon suite. I was watching him through my binoculars and urging Melvin to shoot. He was behind me and to my right so I couldn't see him, but I did hear some commotion. Time was running out. The buck was just a few yards away from thick timber and looking bigger by the second as the shoot-him-before-he-gets-away syndrome sapped my will power. This time I was armed, and even as I urged Melvin to shoot one last time, the rifle was coming to my shoulder.

"Go ahead and shoot him!" Mel shouted.

I did, after which it slowly dawned on me what had happened. My Montana deer season was over. I could only hope that the pent-up frustration and the excitement of the moment hadn't caused me to make a mistake. Happily, when we reached the buck, I saw that he was indeed a good one — a 20-inch 10-pointer scoring 155. I've killed bigger, but I don't recall one that brought more relief and satisfaction.

7:30 p.m. — Upon Melvin's insistence, I hunted with Ed this afternoon. Ed has put forth the effort but hasn't had a crack at anything good all week. It didn't happen this afternoon, either. We managed to see only two small bucks, a handful of does and another moose. There was, however, a lot of sign in the area where I shot the buck this morning. We'll be there at daybreak.

Wednesday, November 24

6:15 a.m. — I've got to go home at noon today and take care of domestic affairs; namely, try to help my wife and two daughters get their bucks. The Thanksgiving hunt has become quite a tradition in our family and is zealously protected and fostered by my lovely wife, Debbie. Ed and I are getting an early start this morning because this is our last shot at a buck. Conditions are perfect, though. It just stopped snowing after dumping another inch. Any deer sign we see will be piping hot.

11:40 a.m. — If "close" counted, we'd be happy hunters. But it doesn't, so our morning ended with yet another sad story about the buck that got away. It wasn't Ed's fault, though. If anyone's, it was mine. Ed wanted something in the 140s, and being from Georgia, he's had little experience judging whitetails of that caliber. Consequently, I told him not to shoot until I gave the go-ahead. Unfortunately, Ed minded a little too well.

Before you ever take to the field, determine what kind of buck you want to shoot and know how to recognize him. Don't wait until a buck is standing in front of you to begin your deliberations. If you do, you run the risk of losing critical seconds, and you may make your decision based on adrenalin rather than reason.

The action started just after first light. After slipping past two does and a yearling buck, we came upon several sets of running-deer tracks. The snow told the story clearly. We could see where the hot doe would stop, then lunge forward as the buck hazed her. Outside the main chase were a couple sets of sizable tracks, undoubtedly belonging to satellite bucks hoping to cut in on the big boy. Most encouraging of all, prints from the tips of some very wide antlers were clearly visible in the snow where the doe had urinated and the buck had lowered his head to sniff. We took up the trail immediately, knowing we were right behind them.

Only a 100 yards down the trail, we came to a sidehill overlooking a stand of young lodgepoles and larch trees. As we looked down the slope for the breeding party, a 115-class 8-pointer darted excitedly through an opening about 125 yards below us. Several more minutes of watching yielded nothing. We could have pursued the party, but I was hesitant to give up the great elevation and sightlines we'd found there. Instead, we'd try to bring them to us, or at least make them show themselves. I positioned Ed to my right behind a small lodgepole and began using my rattling horns to produce the sounds of fighting bucks.

The 8-pointer we had seen earlier responded immediately, bounding straight for us. Ed quickly got into shooting position, but I told him to hold off. The buck was too small. When that deer lost interest, I began rattling again. A minute later, I saw a buck of unknown size coming through the larches to my left. I told Ed another buck was coming in and turned to face the advancing whitetail. I heard Ed shifting behind me and assumed he had also turned to face the deer I was watching. I was wrong.

The buck broke cover about 50 yards in front of me. I was disappointed to see he was a yearling 8-pointer. At that moment, Ed whispered urgently, "Tell me something! Should I shoot?"

I was surprised he couldn't tell the buck was just a yearling. "No," I answered. "He's smaller than the first one."

Ed responded quickly, this time with even more urgency. "No he's not. He's big!"

The realization probably hit Ed and me at the same time — we were looking at different deer! I turned toward Ed as he was spinning my way. We both saw each other's buck at the same time. Ed shouted in a low voice, "Not that one!"

Even as the words left his mouth, I was blurting out, "Shoot him, Ed, shoot him!"

Ed had completed his pivot back toward the buck, which was facing us at 20 yards, and was just shouldering his rifle when the 22-inch 8-pointer wheeled around and vanished into the thick lodgepoles. Ed slumped as though someone had let the air out of him. I was stunned. I tried to make sense of what had just happened . . . not only at that moment, but indeed during the whole week. There were no answers.

Ed and I gave it the old college try the rest of the morning, but to no avail. I sure wanted those guys to get a good buck, but now their trip is over. And also over, I've decided, is my unofficial career as a hunting guide. I just can't take it anymore!

Author's Note: The day after, on Thanksgiving, my daughter, Jennifer, killed a 130-class 8-pointer with one shot. The next day, my wife shot a 9-pointer scoring 135, also with a single shot. I could hardly bring myself to tell Melvin, Ed and Stevie.

CHAPTER SEVEN

Winning On The Road

by Jay Gates

WHEN HUNTERS GET TOGETHER and talk about the great whitetail meccas of North America, you'll hear plenty of discussion about the merits of such legendary spots as Ohio, Kansas, Saskatchewan and Texas. What won't be heard, I can assure you, is any mention whatsoever of central Arizona. I know. I live there. And while we may have great hunting for mule deer and Coues deer, you'll be searching for a long time if you try to locate a big whitetail in Arizona.

That's why I found myself sitting atop a frozen hay bale in South Dakota, huddled against the cold on the final day of my non-resident whitetail hunt. After waiting two years and traveling over 1,000 miles, time was running out. If I didn't get my buck today, it was all over. Tomorrow, I headed back to Arizona.

I could almost hear the clock ticking in the background.

This wasn't an unfamiliar position for me, however. In 25 years of whitetail hunting, I've always found myself hundreds of miles from home with only a few days to get my buck. It's not the easiest or the most relaxing way to hunt, but I consider it a challenge. I've hunted a wide range of places and habitats — all of them west of the Mississippi River — and have managed to take some fine bucks. Doing so, however, has meant developing my own unique approach to "long-distance scouting."

Most hunters, of course, live a lot closer to their hunting grounds than I do. Those guys can keep an eye on the land, search for sheds in the

Hunting far from his home state of Arizona, the author managed to claim the biggest buck in recent memory from south-central South Dakota. The handsome 10-pointer, taken on the last day of the season, netted 165 Boone & Crockett points. Photo courtesy of Jay Gates.

spring, scout throughout the year and even pattern particular bucks if they wish. By the time the season opens, dedicated local hunters can often know exactly where and when to find certain deer.

But, the visiting whitetail hunter isn't afforded these luxuries. He must go beyond basic hunting techniques and learn to think differently if

The river pasture portion of the ranch consists of coulees and cedar breaks that slope gradually toward the Missouri River. Spot-and-stalk or still-hunting tactics are generally used here. Photo by Jay Gates.

he wants to be successful. The way he scouts — the way I've learned to scout — is an entirely different game.

For example, my hunting season begins in January. That's when I begin making telephone calls and lining up hunting areas. I can amass some astronomical telephone bills before it's all over, but the knowledge I gain serves me well. Most of these conversations are with hunting buddies, area game biologists, conservation officers, Forest Service personnel, BLM officials, landowners and ranch foremen. I learn as much as possible about the habitat and the terrain, deer population densities and the age structure of the herd. I try to determine hunting pressure, the top-end potential for big bucks, places to hunt and ways to do it. This "homework" is time well spent. As bits and pieces slowly fall into place, I gain a clearer vision of what to expect and the confidence that's so critical to any hunter — especially one who's never visited his hunting area before.

Once there, success is almost impossible, I've also learned, without flexibility. You simply never know what you may encounter until you actually get into the field and begin to hunt. I believe too many hunters get locked into a single hunting mode, and when they encounter a new territory or new situation, that method simply may not be effective.

By taking notes through years of hunting, I've learned the value of versatility. Sometimes, stand-hunting is obviously the way to go. You can wait over scrapes or rubs, watch feeding or rutting areas, guard watering holes or monitor trails leading to morning bedding areas. Stands work best in dense habitat, or any areas where it's difficult for a hunter to move around silently. In terrain where the cover is less dense and hunters can move quietly, still-hunting can be the answer. This tactic allows you to cover more country and walk up on more deer. But in broken country or mountainous terrain, spot-and-stalk is often the key. Working as a long-distance spy, you can watch various areas from a vantage point, locate a desirable buck and then plan a route of approach to get within shooting distance.

Sometimes, hunters will encounter situations where deer seem to have become invisible, even though their sign is abundant. Generally, that's an indication that the whitetails have become nocturnal and are sitting tight during the day. In this case, a deer drive may be the only way to force whitetails to move during daylight hours. Such drives may be as simple as a single partner walking through a draw while you block an obvious escape trail or as complicated as an elaborate production involving an entire hunting party. If you're alone, you may be reduced to tromping through a creek bed to see what you can kick up.

If the timing is just right and buck:doe ratios are appropriate, rattling and grunting can produce some exciting and spectacular results. Another viable method, particularly on sprawling ranches, is to cover a lot of country by watching for deer as you travel along the roads. On a given hunt, any or all of these tactics may be necessary. Weather changes, unexpected hunting pressure and countless other unforeseen circumstances can easily combine to ruin your original game plan.

If you expect to be successful "on the road," you truly need to become a student of the species. Learn everything you possibly can about whitetails and their habits, such as habitat preferences, life cycles, breeding habits, feeding preferences and so on. The more you know, the easier it is to analyze a given situation and formulate a winning strategy. Much can be learned simply by watching deer from your stand and taking mental notes. In addition, plenty of knowledge is available from other sources. There is a tremendous amount of instructional material available today on deer, including books, magazines and videotapes. You don't have to look long to find plenty of useful information about whitetail biology.

What I'm trying to illustrate is that without some knowledge, an open mind and an ability to adapt to the situation, you're going to be at a disadvantage — especially when you're on unfamiliar turf. Be willing and prepared to try something different than your favorite method. Listen when locals offer advice or talk about strategy. Some of it will be worthless, but then again, you just might learn something. I certainly have. In fact, that's how I found myself hunting in South Dakota.

When you're sitting on a stand, you're wasting time if you're not also analyzing your surroundings. Pay attention to what's going on around you and try to learn from your observations. Why did that doe walk past your stand and not somewhere else? When you saw a buck cross her trail, how did he react to her scent? What's the weather doing and has it changed recently? Store your notes and observations for future reference, and patterns will begin to emerge that will help you in the future.

By listening carefully to Joe Kirwin, who owns a ranch in the south-central portion of the state, I enjoyed a remarkable learning experience and a remarkable hunt. Joe is the type of guy you learn things from. His study of whitetails and their habitats have helped him amass a collection of trophy deer anyone would envy. He's long been managing his ranch and its deer herd to preserve the quality of both the habitat and the hunting.

When I first met Joe in 1983, I had a hard time believing the stories he told me about the South Dakota bucks he'd taken. When he finally showed me photos, my jaw must have hit my chest. The first time Joe killed a buck grossing more than 160 Boone & Crockett points was back in 1970. Of the bucks Joe has taken since then, seven have gross scores between 140 and 150 points, 10 measure between 150 and 160 points and three monsters have tallied between 160 and 170 points. That's a lot of whitetail antlers to have come from 2,300 acres! When he first invited me to hunt on his ranch in 1985, it took me about five seconds to accept.

That first hunt taught me a lot about flexibility and learning to adapt. That's because Joe's ranch is split into three distinct habitat types, all requiring a different hunting approach. First, there's the river pasture, consisting of cedar breaks and coulees that slope gradually into the Missouri River. The north pasture, meanwhile, surrounds a 400-acre federal

Brushy creek bottoms and rolling hills characterize the south pasture of the ranch. Glassing from high vantage points is the best way to find bucks in this region. Photo by Jay Gates.

eagle wildlife refuge and is adjoined by vast acreage of state land that is under cultivation most of the year. Finally, the south pasture is composed of rolling hills and brushy creek bottoms. Each portion is unique.

The agricultural pasture in the north calls for stand-hunting or blind-hunting, both of which allow you to sit and wait for feeding animals or rutting groups that utilize the open country during November. The river pasture is a spot-and-stalk area, featuring plenty of prime glassing sites where you can search for wandering bucks during morning and evening hours. Still-hunting is also a good bet there. In Joe's south pasture, we regularly glass likely areas from the truck, looking for bucks we can stalk (especially if a recent rain will help dampen the sounds of our steps).

In 1986, we used all of these techniques. Joe took another awesome buck, a 7x7 that grossed 168 points and netted 159 after deductions. Joe's son, Jay, tagged an 8-pointer scoring 155 points, and I managed to take a 10-pointer that tallied 135 inches.

Two years later, in 1988, I was fortunate enough to again draw a non-resident South Dakota whitetail license. With great anticipation, I

Joe Kirwin, who owns the 2,300-acre ranch in South Dakota where the author hunted, got things started with this heavy-bodied 10-pointer. It was one of many big bucks he's taken through the years. Photo by Jay Gates.

set out for the ranch in mid-November, hoping the bucks would be rut-crazy when I showed up. After a two-hour drive to Las Vegas from my home, a four-hour flight into Sioux Falls and finally another three-hour drive to Joe's place, I arrived completely exhausted. But, I had a relaxing day before the opener, playing bird dog for a pheasant hunting party that included Joe and Ed Beattie, who I knew from previous mule deer hunts in Wyoming.

On opening day, Joe, his son Jay and I all took different stands on the northern section of the ranch, where we could watch the grain fields. I saw several decent bucks in the 130-inch class during the morning. They were all obviously in full rut, chasing does and doing their best to kill one another, but none of them were big enough to tempt me.

The remainder of the day passed slowly, as we diligently guarded the fields in case a breeding buck decided to pass by. I saw a few more deer as evening came, but none as interesting as the ones I'd seen in the morning. I was still in good spirits, though, as I made my way back to Joe's in the fading light. When I arrived, I was elated to discover that Joe had taken a beautiful, heavy-bodied 10-pointer that scored about 140. Things were definitely off to a fantastic start!

If your goal is to shoot a trophy buck, you must learn to pass up smaller ones. This is a basic premise, of course, but many hunters yield to temptation and end up taking a buck that's smaller than they wanted. If you conclude your hunt early by shooting a small buck, you won't be around when the big one comes by. Know what you want before you begin and stick to your convictions. You may occasionally go home empty-handed, but in the long run, you'll put more trophies on the wall.

Day two began on a promising note, with patchy skies and a light breeze rustling the trees and shrubs. I had situated myself in another of Joe's grain fields in the north pasture, using hay bales to conceal my position. Early in the morning, two bucks passed through separately, seemingly in a hurry to be somewhere else. The first was an unimpressive 8-pointer, measuring perhaps 120 inches, that never slowed down as he crossed the west corner of the field. An hour later another buck appeared, looking somewhat unsure of himself, and milled around in the same area. At about 130 inches, he was bigger than the previous deer but still not a shooter. He fidgeted about, fed briefly and soon went on his way.

I waited through the morning, amid ever-increasing winds. By noon, the sky had turned darker with thick clouds, and it was becoming bitterly cold. It didn't seem as though the deer were moving, so I left the blind.

I spent the rest of the day still-hunting some of the thick draws on the north end of Joe's ranch, moving slowly and glassing frequently. Several times, I walked up on bedded does or kicked unseen deer from heavy cover in front of me. The deer were sitting tight. Toward evening, the weather had turned nasty and I was convinced it was going to snow. Though I hated to waste any time during a short four-day season, I headed to the vehicle an hour before dark and drove back to the warmth of Joe's house. When we compared notes, I learned that we'd all experienced similar situations that day. But, optimisim ran high since we expected the following morning to be ideal from the weather report.

When we awoke early the next morning, we discovered two inches of new snow on the ground and the sky studded with bright stars. The wind had settled down, and the temperature had dropped even farther. With these conditions, I knew I wouldn't want to be confined to a stand since I felt sure the deer would be on the move. I asked Joe to drop me off on the river pasture end of the ranch. When I stepped from the truck, I noticed how soft and quiet the snow felt beneath my feet. I waited for awhile, watching the sun rise through a low haze, before I began still-hunting along the edges of some draws, where I could also keep an eye on the open hillsides. I hadn't gone far when I spotted two immature bucks ahead of me, their little 6-point racks clacking together as they went through the motions of fighting. They seemed unsure about the whole process.

Deeper in the brush, I found a set of impressive whitetail tracks traveling in the same direction I was. I slowed to a crawl and followed them, checking ahead frequently with the binoculars. As I inched my way along, the brush became more dense and I realized my odds of walking up on the buck were slim. So, locating a spot that afforded a good view in two directions, I sat down and dug out the rattling antlers from my pack. The air was completely calm. As I began gently tapping the antlers together, the sound seemed amplified in the still morning air, startling me a bit at first. Thirty minutes of rattling produced nothing, however. By now, the sun had climbed higher and the snow was gradually melting.

Before you head into the field each day, think carefully about the current situation. Ask yourself what the deer are likely to do in these weather conditions, and use your past observations to make the best hunting choice for that day. Don't become a slave to ritual or habit. Think before you start to hunt.

Leaving the buck's tracks, I climbed a slight rise and used my binoculars to scan the surrounding area. That's how I spent the rest of the day. Although I enjoyed being out on

When the cover is too dense for effective still-hunting, rattling may be the best way to bring bucks into view. Joe Kirwin has used this technique with great success on his ranch. Photo by Jay Gates.

foot, free of any schedules or specific plans, I saw only one other buck, a pretty 130-class 10-pointer courting a small group of does on one of the open hillsides.

Suddenly, I was down to the final day of the hunt. I wasn't feeling exactly panicked, because I've taken my share of good bucks and I'd had opportunities to take decent deer on this hunt. But, there is always a certain feeling of anxiety when a season is coming to a close and you may go home empty-handed.

Joe's eight-month-old baby had come up sick during the night, so he was unable to hunt with me the last day. Jay had to go back to school. That left only me. Joe let me borrow his van, and I departed for the field alone at 4:30 in the morning, allowing plenty of time to get to my stand before daylight. The weather remained the same as the day before — clear and cold with no wind — and I couldn't help but think the rut would be in full swing this morning, especially after the passing of the front. Consequently, the fields adjacent to the state game refuge seemed a likely bet. They offered the type of open country rutting deer seem to favor.

Always be prepared to shoot on a moment's notice. Whitetail hunting scenarios usually evolve quickly, and fast reactions can mean the difference between success and failure. It's very easy to "lose your edge" when you spend long periods of time waiting on a stand, but you must focus on being prepared. You may have only a few seconds to make a decision and take a shot.

I was on top of a hay bale long before daylight. It wasn't until 7 o'clock that I could see well enough to perceive deer moving in the fields. I watched as they milled about and fed, occasionally spooking and running a short distance for no apparent reason.

As it grew lighter, I was able to make out a couple of decent 8-pointers mingling with the does. Then, from the state land bordering Joe's property, I saw two does break away and begin running parallel to me, about 200 yards out. They caught my interest immediately, as this type of behavior often signals the arrival of another buck into the area. I studied them carefully, wondering if another hunter had spooked them or if there was really a buck in pursuit.

I didn't have to wait long for an answer. A whitetail buck abruptly bounded into view, his nose to the ground, trailing like a hound. Even at that distance, there was no question about him. He was huge! With no need to evaluate his rack any further, I quickly set my binoculars aside, grabbed my rifle and found a shooting rest. The buck was moving briskly to my right through some scattered brush, and he would disappear into thick timber with a few more steps. I swung the crosshairs with him and squeezed the trigger.

There was no smack of bullet against bone. Though it hadn't sounded good, I still waited ... for 20 long minutes. A 20-month stretch in jail would have passed more quickly.

Finally, when I felt enough time had passed, I climbed down from my hay bale to search for blood. When I reached the area, I could find no sign that the buck had actually existed, much less been hit. There was nothing.

I decided I needed help. Two days earlier, I had met a friendly local game warden, and since he knew the country almost as well as Joe, I decided I'd ask him to help me look for the buck. When he and I returned to the scene, I was almost embarrassed that I hadn't looked harder. It took us only five minutes to locate the buck. And wow, what a buck!

With 10 long tines, massive main beams and nine-inch eyeguards, he was as beautiful a whitetail as I had ever seen, and by far the best I had ever taken. After digging out a tape and carefully measuring him, I came up with a gross score of 168 B&C points and a net tally of 165. Not only was he my best whitetail, but he was also the biggest buck that had been taken in the area for as long as anyone could remember. The warden told me the buck was the best he had ever seen.

Never, never assume you have missed a deer, no matter how dismal the situation appears after the shot. You owe it to the animal to make every effort to determine whether or not it's been hit. If you discover you did make a hit, it's your responsibility to do everything possible to recover that animal. Always examine the area where the buck was standing, even if you are certain you've missed the shot.

When I arrived at Joe's house a short time later and showed him my buck, he nearly came apart at the seams! He couldn't have been happier for me. Friends and game wardens from three surrounding counties began arriving to admire the buck, and I realized how fortunate I had been to come this far from home and take such a remarkable trophy. In more than a quarter century of hunting different kinds of deer, this buck will always be one of my all-time favorites. I couldn't have asked for a more memorable hunt, or better friends than the Kirwins. I'd traveled a long ways from Arizona, but it sure felt like home.

CHAPTER EIGHT

Saskatchewan's Wild-Card Buck

by Jim Shockey

THE SUN HOVERED JUST ABOVE THE HORIZON, suspended in a gray sky. Stretched out before me, a frozen field sported its wheat-stubble beard, now blanketed in white frost. And up above, a cold ice fog slowly began to drift across the landscape. I shivered.

I'd been sitting in the same spot for nearly six hours, not hunting exactly, just sitting, waiting, biding my time. All day there had been no wind, not a breath, and now almost imperceptibly the ice fog above me began to creep and crawl. Formed when the frigid November air encountered the warmer spring water in a nearby partially frozen river, the fog hung over the countryside like a giant wind indicator. And now, after six hours, the ice fog started to move ... the wrong way.

The wind grew from a gentle puff to a breeze. My hunting plan, like a house of cards, was beginning to tremble. Finally, as the wind swelled in its intensity, my house of cards shuddered, quaked and then collapsed around me. My plan, the one I'd started constructing more than a year ago, was destroyed. Now, I had to pick up those cards and make a decision.

Hold? Move? Fold?

Bitterly cold (actually, more bitter than cold), I mentally worked through my options. I suddenly realized that I'd believed so strongly in my strategy that I'd never formulated a contingency plan. Now, I had no choice. I had to pick a card and rely on luck.

The plan should have worked. The wind always blew one direction

A last-second ploy by the author gave him the opportunity to take this huge Saskatchewan whitetail with a muzzleloader. The trophy buck grossed over 170 Boone & Crockett points and wound up with a net typical score of 167 1/8. Photo courtesy of Jim Shockey.

in the latter part of November. Always. And for me to have any chance of killing a big buck in that spot, it was imperative that the wind behave as it should. That's because the deer, which numbered upwards of 100 on some evenings, always emerged from the forest in one particular area and then travelled through the burn for a full half-mile before entering the field at dark to feed.

I'd watched them do it three days in a row the year before. On the fourth evening, I'd set up to intercept them, and on that evening some slob — a poacher actually, because he certainly didn't have permission to hunt there — roared across the burn in a 4-wheel drive pickup truck. He then jumped out and fired at the first group of deer just as they stepped out from the forest. He missed, they ran, he jumped in his truck and roared back across the burn. I called it a year. There was only one day left in the season anyway, and after that, I was too disgusted to hunt.

That had been a year ago, and since then, not a day had passed when I didn't think of that hunt and my plan. Months before this season, I called the landowner to confirm both my intent to hunt his land again and his intent to allow me. During the summer months I phoned him often, always asking about the burn, the forest and the field. Every time I asked, he confirmed the deer were still there, still leaving the forest before last light, still travelling through the burn and still feeding in the field. In the morning, they did the same thing in reverse order. One evening, he counted 200 deer.

Choosing the right place and the right time to hunt can, and should, be done prior to the hunting season. Picking where to go, what to do, where to sit, where to rattle, where to walk, where to wait and what to take can all be predetermined. By having a strategy, you'll save valuable time and make the most of your hunt.

During those months prior to the season, I formulated my plan, analyzed every detail, thought out every possibility (I thought) and slowly built my house of cards. I wasn't going to make the 1,000-mile journey to Saskatchewan and, once there, rely strictly on luck. No, I had a plan.

The last consideration, the final card on my house, had been a face card — and the face was that of the wind. It had to blow from one of three directions. If it didn't, it would mean certain failure. But for that to happen, the wind would have to do something it simply never did. Mentally, I placed the final card on the house, confident that my plan was solid.

A solid game plan, based on pre-season scouting, is the best way to prepare for a hunt. But, even the most carefully considered strategy is no more stable than a house of cards. At some point in every hunt, you're liable to encounter unexpected variables that may be beyond your control. When that happens, your own knowledge, resourcefulness, intuition and luck will determine the outcome.

Now, on the afternoon of the first day, the wind was doing the unthinkable. It was blowing in the wrong direction! I had to make a choice, but I found it difficult to do. It was far easier to just postpone picking a card, postpone the possibility of failing. The ice fog roiled over me, billowing toward the forest. I hunched lower in my blanket, shivered some more and, rather than choose a new course of action, decided instead to review the morning's

Hidden in the cover on top of a small hill, the author overlooked an open field similar to this one. From his vantage point, he watched more than 80 whitetails parade past. The biggest buck was the only deer that was beyond his shooting range! Photo by Jim Shockey.

events and search for clues that might tell me what to do next.

It was pitch-black and eerily still when I parked my truck off the side of the grid road that morning. By flashlight, I readied my equipment, including my Knight muzzleloader, my possibles bag, my boot blankets and a regular blanket. I pulled on layer after layer of clothing. Sixty hours earlier, I'd been a thousand miles away, languishing in the relative warmth and security of my home on Vancouver Island off British Columbia. Now, as I hopped around trying to pull my moccasin rubbers over thick wool socks, the Island seemed a million miles away.

Every fibre in my body seemed to vibrate, both in anticipation of the hunt and because of all the caffeine in my system. I started shivering the instant I stepped from the cab of the truck, but by the time I had all the clothes on, I was hot, sweaty and in a hurry. Still, I had to be sure I brought everything I needed. From experience, I knew how easy it was to forget something in the dark. I ran through my mental checklist one last time.

It was on that last check that I remembered my rattling antlers. In

Snow and heavy frost usually blanket the northern extremes of the whitetail's range, and Saskatchewan certainly is no exception. While the extreme cold can make hunting difficult, the snow can also make it easier to spot and track deer. Photo by Jim Shockey.

10 years of serious whitetail hunting in Saskatchewan and Alberta, I've rattled in a grand total of five bucks. Only five. This in spite of hearing from a dozen hunters how effective rattling whitetails in the north country can be. Still, in spite of my personal lack of success, I make it a point to carry my rattling antlers whenever I hunt whitetails. If nothing else, they make me look like I know what I'm doing.

Fifteen minutes after stepping from my truck and with an hour to go before daylight, I shuffled off toward the trailhead I'd discovered the year before. It was an old cart trail, an ice trail maybe, but whatever it was, it led through the forest directly to the old burned-off block. Where it had been black and silent before, it was now black and noisy. Each step I took sounded like a squeaking floor in a haunted house. I was concerned that the deer, still a mile away through solid forest, would hear me. My concern was unfounded, of course, but when you slip through a black forest, it doesn't matter that there is nothing there to hear you or mark your passage. Something inside you — a leftover predatory instinct, perhaps — commands you to go in silence.

I tried walking on my tiptoes, which did help but not significantly. The air was too cold and too still. Somewhere off to my side, maybe 20 yards away, an unknown creature crunched off into the blackness. I cursed under my breath and continued, gritting my teeth at each noisy step. It didn't matter what animals I scared off in the forest, I told myself. I had no choice, anyway. I had to go through the forest to get to the burn and intercept the deer as they traveled from the field.

Sound travels easily and quickly through frozen air, sometimes confusing our perceptions of what is near and far. Be aware of this when hunting in cold climates, and remember that the sounds you hear are probably farther away from you than they seem to be.

There was a hill in the center of the burn, more like a bald knob, actually, and from there, I knew I would have a commanding view of the mile-long by half-mile-wide burn. I needed to see with my own eyes where the deer exited the field and which routes they traversed through the burn's saplings. Standing within those finger-thick saplings you might expect to see clearly for 100 yards and recognize forms at 150 yards. But from up on my knob, I knew I would be able to see down into the saplings and spy on the deer as they made their way toward the forest. The wind was not a factor — it never was in the morning at that time of the year. A calm always pervades the winter dawn on this very northern edge of the whitetail's range. You can count on it. I did.

If I felt hot back at the truck, I was near meltdown by the time I completed the mile walk along the narrow, snow-covered trail. It isn't good to work up such a sweat before a long sit in the cold, but I had no choice. The ribbon-like trail winding off into the blackness before me was beginning to fade. Where it had once stood out in sharp contrast to its surroundings, it now seemed as though I was walking on the back of a dull grey snake. I had to hurry.

The deer, at least those of the previous year, fed in the field all night and then, at the first hint of morning, moved off the field and into the relative security of the burn. There they did their deer thing until midmorning, slowly drifting toward the safety of the forest. It was vital that I reach the knob before the deer left the field.

Recall is a wonderfully selective thing. As I write this, I clearly remember all the good things, like reaching the knob. I do not, however, clearly recall the frantic rush, the ragged breathing and the fear of a spoiled hunt due to a miscalculated and therefore late morning start. I do recall, quite vividly, the first deer stepping slowly toward my vantage point within minutes of my arrival. I do not, however, have a good recollection of all the shadowy forms that floated away from my dark approach, ethereal shapes betrayed only by the staccato sounds of their hooves fleeing across the frozen ground.

Picking the exact spot where you will set up is critical to success. Besides anticipating the direction of the wind, you should also anticipate from which direction the deer will approach. Make sure you consider not only your ability to see the deer, but also the deer's ability to see you.

To keep my location secret, I hid on the forest side of the knob. From there I would see any deer that passed by a half-mile to either side of my location. Until they passed, the deer wouldn't be able to see me, and even then, they could do so only if they looked back. It was part of my plan, my carefully constructed house of cards. For a year, I'd seen in my mind's eye exactly what I was seeing that morning. One factor I had not reckoned with was the noisy snow, but now that I was sitting still and the deer were moving, that factor was in my favor.

As it grew light, I could hear the deer approaching my hill. Though I dared not poke my head over to look, it seemed a certainty that they would pass on both sides of me. I expected the first of the deer to appear within easy shooting range, at about 100 yards. But when I finally saw them, they were more like 200 yards away.

Farther down the burn, three more deer crossed my line of sight but still no bucks. Closer by, another group crossed to the forest, stopping for a moment before jumping over the three-strand barbed-wire fence. Again, no bucks. Then, six deer showed with another following close behind, nose to the ground. A small buck. No, two small bucks, both intent on the group of does.

For the next 45 minutes, the deer streamed by in ones, twos and groups of up to eight. As each deer crossed into my sight, my heart would pound a beat or two faster until I saw there was no big buck among them. Finally, I noticed movement at the extreme edge of my vision, near the

Just in time, some almost-forgotten rattling antlers gave the author his chance to take this 5x5 typical trophy. Both of the deer's main beams exceeded 25 inches in length, and its longest tine measured 12 4/8 inches. Photo by Jim Shockey.

point where the burn joined the horizon. My heart pounded, and this time, it kept pounding as I raised my binoculars.

The buck was a black-horned thug, neck swelled and spoiling for a fight. I didn't need optics to tell that he thought he was tough. This buck swaggered. My binoculars confirmed what I suspected. He was big, apparently a 4x4 with 12-inch tines on each side. With any mass at all, he'd score near 160 gross Boone and Crockett points.

I watched the buck work through the burn, cutting toward the forest on a course that would bring him within 600 yards of me at the closest point. Occasionally, I would lower my binoculars to watch other, closer deer still streaming by, but there were none to compare to the brute crossing the burn.

At the fence, the buck stopped and stood with his head down for nearly a full minute. Then, with a fluid leap, he was over the fence and vanished from sight. He was gone, but other deer still filtered by for the next hour. It was nearly midmorning when the curtain fell and the show ended.

Over the course of those two hours, to the best of my recollection,

Five days after the author claimed his first trophy, he hunted the other side of the nearby river and took a second big buck with his muzzleloader. This one netted 166 5/8 net B&C points as a non-typical. Photo by Jim Shockey.

about 80 deer passed through the burn and into the forest. Eight were bucks, and I could have killed any one of them except the big one. The second-largest was a respectable 130 B&C buck, but the others were unremarkable. Not a bad morning to be sure, but most importantly, I knew the big buck was there.

All was well in my house of cards.

My strategy had been to wait every day on the knob until I saw a trophy-class buck. Once I did, I'd planned to set up on him. It was that simple. All I had to was wait.

And wait I did.

For six hours, I'd been waiting patiently. For six hours, the ice fog had hovered over my head, and then, against the prevailing wind pattern, the fog began to drift. The wind was blowing directly into the forest! One minute all was well and going according to plan, and the next, my carefully laid plans came tumbling down.

The wind began shifting back and forth, scattering my scent in every imaginable direction throughout the forest. If the buck was there, he would smell me. If the buck was there, he would know.

If the buck was there.

Time was running short. There was no more time to analyze and think about the morning's events. I had to move, had to make a decision. Nothing was clear any longer, not like before the season.

I picked a card.

Never quit scouting, even after you begin to hunt. Sometimes, by looking at an area from a different perspective, you can notice features or options that weren't previously apparent. Keep your eyes and your mind open to new possibilities.

Without knowing why exactly, I gathered my gear and stood up on numbed legs. To say that I made the choice to get up and walk over to where the buck entered the forest six hours earlier based on sound logic would be like saying I believed it was possible to build a card house in a hurricane. The wind was all wrong to hunt that spot. Logic dictated that I leave the area, wait until tomorrow and hope for a more favorable wind. But, logic had nothing to do with my choice. I was playing cards now.

The buck's tracks were right where they should have been, but the facts of the situation were not computing. From where I'd been sitting on the knob, I felt like I was in the perfect place for an ambush. But now, it didn't feel right. So, I moved farther from the knob. Again, the decision wasn't a conscious one. I simply moved.

Farther down the fenceline, without warning, the burn abruptly dropped away into a deep ravine. Because of the lighting or the angle, I'd been unable to see it from my vantage point on the knob. It was there I stopped. Turning my head, I looked several hundred yards up the ravine and saw movement. At first, I didn't look closely, feeling that perhaps it was a coyote. But after watching for a moment, I realized there was something familiar in the way the animal moved. I lifted my binoculars.

For the second time that day, my heart started pounding and didn't stop. Because for the second time, the dark-horned buck was making his way out of the burn. He was using the contours of the land to his best advantage — keeping low, staying out of sight and moving quickly. He had obviously used a similar maneuver to avoid detection when he slipped out of the forest, unseen by me, sometime during the past six hours.

Staying out of range of my muzzleloader, the buck worked his way over to the opposite side of the ravine, 400 yards away. From there, he could climb over the edge of the ravine and into the forest. If the wind had been blowing the direction it should have been, he would have already detected me. But it wasn't. I didn't purposely plan to head to a position downwind from the buck. I just did. I just played another card.

While the buck made his way along the far side of the ravine toward the forest, I sorted through my possible choices. There were so many! Drop down into the ravine and try to head him off? Slip into the forest and work my way through it to intercept him there? Wait and do nothing, hoping he'd come back this way? I was frozen by indecision, unable to decide which card to turn over. Time was running out.

The buck, now at the edge of the forest, jumped the fence and began to melt away. He was changing from a whole deer into just bits and glimpses, merging with the perimeter trees and dissolving into the heart of the forest. I was frantic. I was losing him! The cards had all disappeared, save one. In desperation, I grabbed hold of the rattling antlers I'd almost forgotten that morning — the rattling antlers that had been hitching a free ride around my neck for 10 years, little more than freeloading bums. I hit them together. Instantly, the buck slammed on the brakes and stopped. As he did, he magically blended into the background, becoming impossible to see. When I stopped rattling the antlers, the buck came back to life, literally leaping toward me, running now at full tilt!

I threw the antlers to the side, right into the strands of the barbed-wire fence. They swung and clanked against each other as I scrambled to ready my rifle, snagging my jacket on the wire and ripping it as I did. The wire twanged loudly and set the antlers to swinging again. At the bottom of the ravine, the buck stopped, listening intently to the new sounds. It was then I noticed he was a 5x5 and probably a gross 170-plus buck. Heck, maybe even a 170 net buck. But, I was judging instead of shooting. There was one more card to play.

The shot would have been too long and too rushed. I waited. The buck was running again now, and he disappeared below me as he ran onto my side of the ridge. Without thinking, I dropped to my knees, rested my muzzleloader against a fencepost and waited for him to appear over the ridge.

Seconds later he did, bursting toward me, head-on and at full speed. I will never forget the explosive power in those shoulders as he stormed over the edge of the ravine 30 yards away and into my sights. Nor will I ever forget the stare of intent in his eye.

I'd like to be able to say I consciously squeezed off a well-planned shot, but I'd be lying if I did. I saw brown and yanked the trigger. It was just another lucky card.

The buck never knew what hit him.

Chapter Nine

The Ghost Of Boggy Slough

by Dr. James C. Kroll

THE FIRST TIME I SAW THE GHOST, I had no way of knowing how strangely intertwined our two lives would become.

I was a young biologist conducting a habitat study in a steamy swamp of the Cochina Bayou in East Texas. He was a yearling buck, perhaps the ugliest deer I had ever seen, but full of fight. When I stumbled upon him in the summer of 1982, he was trying mightily to work over a big tree with his small, misshapen antlers. Suddenly, he looked up and stared straight at me. For a few moments, we both stood motionless, sizing up one another. Then he snorted, wheeled around and ran off.

I didn't pay much attention to that encounter at the time. After all, as a whitetail biologist and researcher, I had studied countless deer. But, this buck would turn out be something special. For five remarkable years, as the yearling gradually grew into a mature buck, our paths would cross again and again. Fate, it seemed, kept bringing us together.

My interest was professional as well as personal. After all, I'd spent years studying deer and their habitat in Boggy Slough as part of an extensive research project. By placing radio collars on the deer and tracking them with telemetry, I'd been spying on bucks as they traveled about the forests, learning how they reacted not only to each other but to hunting pressure as well. Though I captured and collared many bucks during the study, the Ghost — as he came to be known — was never one of them.

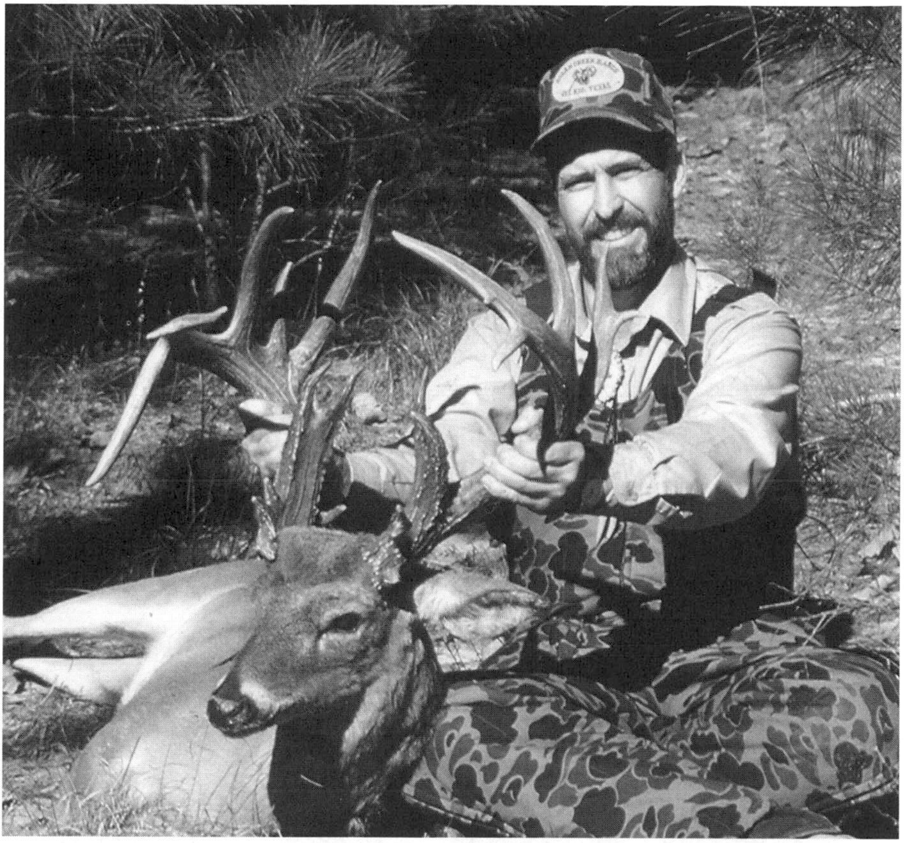

After watching the buck grow up over a six-year period, the author finally claimed the East Texas non-typical in 1987. The giant whitetail netted an impressive 190 3/8 Boone & Crockett points. Photo by Matt Williams.

For some reason, I just enjoyed knowing he was there. Through the years, we kept tabs on one another.

Boggy was a fascinating place to study deer, partly because of its unusual history. Originally purchased by T.L.L. Temple as part of his timber empire, it soon became a popular hunting spot. Temple, along with a Captain Ray, fenced the entire area to keep out hogs, and then fiercely protected the resident deer herd from dog hunting and poaching.
Without knowing it, Temple and Ray had produced a unique biological situation.

There are some 30 races of whitetails in North America, and perhaps the largest — in terms of antler size — is the Kansas race, Odocoileus virginianus macrourus. Although few people realize it, this same Kansas

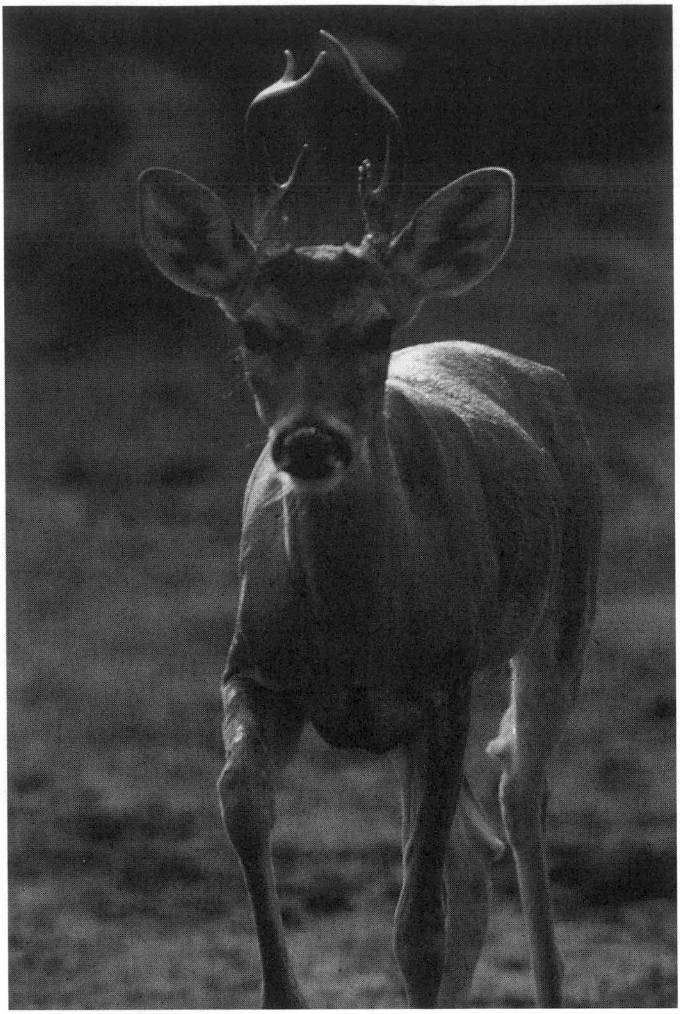

When the Ghost was an 18-month-old yearling, the author rattled him in and snapped this photograph. The young buck's rack gave little indication of how impressive it would eventually become. Photo by Dr. James C. Kroll.

race once inhabited much of what is now the Pineywoods region of East Texas. The protected deer herd at Boggy, I believe, is an isolated remnant of that race. And, the heart of that herd lives in the Cochina Bayou near the Neches River, where I was doing my research.

Boggy was special to me for other reasons as well. It was my work there that opened the door for some new concepts in deer behavior, including the importance of signposts (later documented by Dr. R. Larry Marchinton at the University of Georgia). This East Texas "workshop" also helped me discover and study the sanctuary and travel corridor concepts. And, it was at Boggy that I learned about the unpredictable movement patterns of mature bucks.

It was a signpost that first introduced me to the Ghost, because he was tearing up one of my study trees that first day I saw him. Over the

A signpost is a specialized rub created by a dominant buck when he rubs his antlers and head against a tree. Secretions from the gland in his forehead contain a chemical that serves two purposes — one, makes does more receptive to breeding and, two, suppresses the breeding behavior of subordinate bucks. Signposts are strategically placed, usually in sanctuaries or staging areas, and are frequented by does and other bucks. Unlike common rubs, a signpost is used for communication, not exercise.

next few weeks, I spotted the young whitetail often, and even had the chance to photograph him once. I decided to keep an eye on this upstart buck, and each time I returned to the area, I'd find a new rub. He actually began to make a nuisance of himself as, one by one, my study trees succumbed to his onslaught! From the beginning, I took a special interest in the Ghost.

As it turned out, that deer's behavior — observed through several years — provided me with a textbook example of how to pattern a buck and how to use that information to develop a sound hunting plan. And in the end, the Ghost also wound up providing one of my greatest thrills.

I quickly discovered that the Ghost had three distinct habitat preferences. First, deep in the Cochina swamp, he maintained a summer sanctuary located on a small island that remained dry even during the heaviest of flooding. It was no more than 100 feet in diameter, but it had all the classic components of a sanctuary, including good screening cover and adequate escape routes.

There was simply no way for a man to approach this summer hideout without being detected. Whenever I returned to measure my vegetation plots, he would slip away long before I could get near the tiny island. On several occasions, however, I would outsmart him by positioning myself along one of his travel corridors while an assistant approached the study area. Each time, I was able to remain undetected while I witnessed the buck quietly exit the area. Because he was accustomed to me and I didn't make a pest of myself, he tolerated my occasional intrusions and remained in the area.

The second habitat he favored was a young pine plantation bordering the edge of the swamp. The third habitat was a mixed pine and hardwood stand that provided escape from the summer heat and a variety of foods in both summer and fall.

In 1983, a year after I first saw the Ghost, I was back in the swamp studying my plots. To my frustration, I discovered that a buck had set up shop in the area and was destroying all the vegetation with his rubbing. He seemed particularly fond of sweetleaf and holly trees. One day while approaching the area, I heard some telltale rubbing sounds. Slipping in quietly, I spotted the culprit. It was that ugly buck again! But now, at two years of age, he didn't look so laughable. He sported some prominent drop tines on one side and a small kicker on the other. His antler mass was considerable for such a young animal.

Whitetail cover comes in two "flavors." The first is overhead or insulation cover, which protects deer from climatic extremes such as excessive heat or cold. Second is horizontal or screening cover, which gives deer places to hide from predators, including man. The type of cover a deer selects depends upon the time of year. It makes little sense, for example, for a buck to spend much time during mid-summer in a dense pine thicket where there is little wind movement to cool him. An open stand of oaks with little underbrush, on the other hand, provides excellent summer bedding because it offers shade while allowing breezes to penetrate. In winter, of course, those same qualities would make the oak stand an undesirable cover.

I realized that, whether by design or just good fortune, the Ghost had chosen to spend his time in a "safe" area located right between the two hunting clubs in Boggy Slough. This area was unhunted by either club, and I secretly hoped this interesting buck would survive the season.

In the following years, I tried to keep an eye out for the Ghost, but he became more and more difficult to spot. When the rut arrived, though, I began finding his rubs right in the middle of my study area. And each year, those rubs became larger and larger. In 1984, when I caught a glimpse of him near my plots, the sight of his rack almost took my breath away. At 3 1/2 years old, he had transformed himself into a handsome buck that may have been the biggest on the entire property.

I saw him only once in 1985. Just prior to the hunting season, I hid myself in the bottomland and began rattling. The big buck charged in at full speed, ears back and hair standing on end. I was awestruck at the size of his rack! Surely, I thought, he would fall to a hunter that year. But

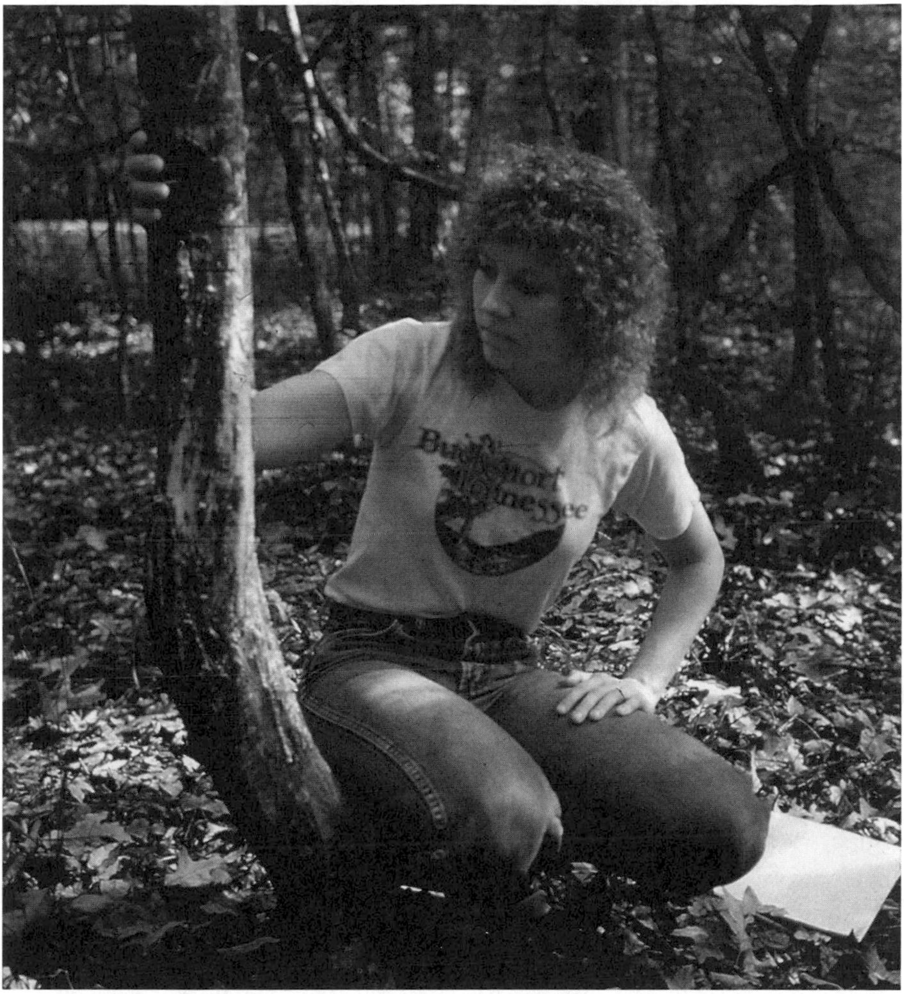

Through the years, the Ghost made a habit of destroying the author's study trees. Here, research assistant Pam Behrmann examines one of the deer's signposts in Boggy Slough. Photo by Dr. James C. Kroll.

when the season was over, the Ghost wasn't among the casualties. He had eluded everyone again.

But in 1986, when I returned to my old study plots in September, I found no sign of the Ghost. He didn't show in October either, and by November, I was convinced that he had died, probably of old age or common post-rut mortality. He also could have moved, because his favorite pine/hardwood stand had been cut that year. Even though the foresters had left enough trees to preserve suitable streamside management zones

Most hunters do their scouting in late summer or early fall, when deer are seen mostly at dawn and dusk as they head out to feed in the evening and return to their bedding areas in the early morning. My research has shown that heavily hunted whitetails, however, are virtually nocturnal. Bucks, especially the mature ones, tend to move at two times — during the night and during midday hours. Does are likewise active at night, but later in the season when food becomes scarce, they will also move during much of the day. Many hunters mistakenly base their hunting schedule on the does' activity patterns, not the buck's.

(SMZs), it may have been too much disturbance for the Ghost.

Was he still out there, I wondered, somehow hidden in the sanctuary of his swamp? Had the Ghost of Boggy Slough finally moved on? Or worse yet, had he passed on, the victim of a hunter from one of the neighboring deer camps? After all these years, I wondered if I'd ever know what became of him.

In the summer of 1987, I received an excited call from Bill Goodrum, another biologist at Boggy Slough. "I've got something you may be interested in," he said coyly.

When I arrived, he pushed a huge shed antler into my face and told me his men had found it the bottomland. It was magnificent, with five perfect points and a seven-inch base. We scored the antler and determined that if the other side of the rack was the same as this one, we were looking at what could have been a 200-inch Boone & Crockett typical!

Bucks and does actually prefer different habitats, so much so that they might as well be different species. Why? It's because bucks gravitate to the poorer habitat, thereby leaving the best food for does and fawns, helping guarantee fawn survival. Hunters must remember this. Too many hunters focus on areas where they've seen large numbers of does instead of seeking out thicker "buck" cover with less desirable food sources.

HT4

I gradually realized, however, that this was not the shed of the buck I'd watched all those years. But, it did share some of the same rack characteristics — enough so to believe that he and the Ghost were genetically related. An intense search for more sheds produced several giant antlers. None were a match to the first shed, but they all had somewhat similar configurations. Apparently, there was more than one monster buck in Boggy Slough.

The 1987 hunting season began with tremendous expectations. Word of the sheds had spread quickly, and both hunting camps were buzzing with talk of world record bucks. Unfortunately, I was unable to hunt the most productive time in East Texas, which is the first week of the season. Years of research had taught me that the primary rut in the area occurs during the last week of October through the first week of November. At least that's true for the Pineywoods in general, but not necessarily for these deer. These animals were related to the Kansas race, and those deer are known to be mid to late-November breeders.

To pattern whitetails, you need to understand their breeding behavior. Unfortunately, the common perception is that bucks are rubbing, scraping, fighting, calling and breeding all at the same time. The truth is there is a predictable and logical progression to all these behaviors, and each one marks a specific stage in the process that we call "the rut." There is a distinct rubbing period when bucks rub trees and saplings to strengthen their neck muscles for the upcoming combat. Next comes signpost construction. Scraping activity then follows during the "late pre-rut" period, marking the time when bucks are most aggressive and likely to fight. Breeding is next, which completes the first true estrus cycle.

The North Boggy Slough Hunting and Fishing Club is responsible for some 700 man-days of hunting pressure every season. Since guests are discouraged from shooting young bucks, the quality of the bucks harvested remains quite high in spite of this heavy pressure. After each hunt that year, I called to see if anyone had taken the monster deer whose shed antler we had found. But when no giant was claimed in the first half of the season, interest began to wane.

My opportunity to hunt came in mid-December. At the club, invited guests draw numbers from a hat, which determines the order in which they may select their hunting spots. I drew No.17 out of 24, but to my surprise, no one ahead of me chose the Cochina Creek bottom area. I did, figuring that if the monster buck who dropped that antler was still alive, he would have a sanctuary near the bottomland. Several hunters, however, had tried the area earlier in the season without success. I knew there wasn't a great chance to find that buck this late in the season, but when I went to bed the evening before the hunt, I still felt I'd made the right decision.

When deer herds are in good physical condition, the first breeding cycle occurs within a period of two weeks or less, when the most dominant does are bred. A second, lesser period of activity occurs 25 days later, when younger does reach estrus. A third very brief estrus may follow in another 25 days as a few fawns and later yearlings are bred. In many herds, though, these periods will overlap one another. Between each of these rut cycles, there are "mini-periods" of rubbing, signpost working and scraping.

That night, a brilliant bolt of lightning illuminated the ceiling over my bunk, awakening me from my sleep. Startled, I peered between the blinds at the menacing storm outside. An intense cold front had moved in unexpectedly after midnight. "Well, there go my chances," I said.

But when I arose well before dawn and eased out onto the porch of the Boggy Slough lodge, a light, cold breeze hit me as I faced north. Above, the stars seemed to be so close I could touch them. My entire attitude changed at that moment — I had a chance after all! In fact, everything was perfect. We had ideal rut conditions for the South (between 30 and 40 degrees, according to my research), with a light three to five-mile-per-hour wind and humidity less than 50 percent. In addition, it was December 18, almost exactly 25 days since the peak of the rut — time for the secondary rut to kick in. All I had to do was decide upon the location and the tactic.

I huddled with Oscar Rogers, one of the Boggy guides and one of the most knowledgeable woodsmen in the area. Picking a location would be tricky. We didn't believe the bucks would approach one of the established stands since my research has indicated that permanent stands are bad ideas for trophy hunters. We also knew that all of the sheds we'd found had been within two miles of the Ghost's old summer sanctuary. Finally, I decided to hunt one of the SMZs that led away from the swamp bottom and into the same 10-year-old pine plantation the Ghost had used as a breeding-season sanctuary. Good buck habitat is good buck habitat, I thought to myself. If the Ghost had liked it, surely this new buck would, too. Besides, the acorn crop was heavy in the Cochina bottom, so the does

With eight-inch bases and four drop tines, the trophy buck grossed over 200 B&C points. He was fooled by the author's grunt calls on a mid-December hunt. Photo by Dr. James C. Kroll.

were probably traveling there to feed.

The next step was to decide on an approach. The wind posed a problem here. Coming out of the north, it would blow my scent straight into the sanctuary pines. If I approached along a feeder of the SMZ, it would allow me to travel most of the way across the wind. But I would have to wait until there was enough daylight; otherwise, I would undoubtedly make too much noise if I tried to stumble through the woods in the dark. This was thick cover, and I would be no more than 100 yards away from the Ghost's old sanctuary.

Oscar drove me from the lodge to my destination near the feeder drainage. As we approached the spot, he simply slowed down and I slipped off the back of his truck.

Moving quietly in the predawn light, I noticed a line of rubs leading up the SMZ toward the pine plantation. Farther along, I spotted a fresh scrape. It had obviously been worked very early that morning, after the midnight rain had ended. I was clearly dealing with a nocturnal buck. My hope now was that he had not located a doe that morning. If he was in that sanctuary with a doe, there would be no way I could lure him out.

About 100 yards from the plantation, the dense vegetation began to open up a bit and I started looking for a hunting spot. Hunters often like to position themselves so they can see several hundred yards, but few trophy bucks will venture very far into such open expanses. I moved a short distance away from the rub line I'd been following and settled in beside a large oak tree. The visibility was only about 40 yards, but that was fine with me. I still had no way of knowing if the rub line belonged to the big buck whose sheds we'd found, or just another eight-pointer. But, I was ready to find out.

After the signpost period, bucks position themselves so that does must move past them on their way to feed. These "staging areas" are adjacent to feeding sites and usually offer plenty of overhead cover with little screening. A mature buck generally moves to his "station" just before darkness and remains there, surrounded by his signposts, throughout the night. During the day, he'll bed down in his sanctuary, which is usually located nearby.

It was time to "match the hatch" by adapting my tactics to fit the deer's current behavior. With the second rut cycle underway, I decided I'd try to lure the buck from his sanctuary. The wind wasn't perfect, however, and I knew he would try to approach downwind. That prompted me to consider a tactic I seldom rely upon — using rutting buck lure. I had a concoction of tarsal gland extract that I'd made a few days earlier by immersing a mature buck's tarsal glands in glycerin, then storing it in my freezer. I poured the concoction all around me.

I had left my rattling horns behind, figuring they would be useless at this point of the season. Instead, I decided it was time to use a grunt call, a technique that has worked very effectively for me through the years.

Raising the call to my mouth, I cupped my hands over its end and gave three short grunts. I listened and watched. I was about to raise the call to my mouth again when it happened.

Charging down the path toward me was a freight train with antlers, a rampaging buck carrying a massive rack with tines that seemed to jut out in every direction. By the time I threw the 7mm Rem. Mag. Ruger to my shoulder, he had slammed on the brakes, just 10 yards away. All I could see through my 6X scope was brown! There was no time to deliberate or analyze, only to react.

Finding what I thought was the right spot, I squeezed the trigger just as the buck turned to run. It all happened so quickly — perhaps in less than two seconds — that I didn't even give thought to what a magnum bullet might do at that short range.

The buck wheeled and ran back into the pines, but the telltale dragging right front leg indicated a mortal wound. I waited several minutes, then followed. The bright red blood trail, along with some bone from his front leg, convinced me the buck would die quickly. But, he was nowhere to be found! I grew extremely anxious over the next hour as I followed the blood trail. The thought of not finding a wounded buck — any buck — troubled me deeply. I had been fortunate to have never lost a deer, but I feared the percentages were catching up with me.

Finally, the sight of those big tines sticking up out of the grass allowed me to breathe once more. In spite of a broken shoulder, pierced lungs and a damaged heart, he had managed to run more than 400 yards into the plantation. He was lying dead next to a signpost. He'd made it all the way back to his sanctuary before collapsing. Then came the real surprise.

It was the Ghost! I could not believe my eyes. Suddenly, I didn't know how I should feel. On the one hand, I had just taken a monster buck with eight-inch bases and four drop tines. At the same time, I had just claimed my old friend, the Ghost.

As I sat beside the now-familiar buck, I remembered the first time I saw him — a homely little yearling with misshapen antlers, flailing away at a tree much too large for him. I also thought about all those times I secretly wished he would go unharmed during the hunting season. To this day, I really don't know exactly how I feel about it all. But, I do know that for six years I'd been haunted by the Ghost and our two lives had become interwoven in the Pineywoods of East Texas. Every time I look up at that magnificent head on my wall, I remember how a young buck and a young biologist grew up together. I will be forever grateful.

CHAPTER TEN

A Father's Greatest Trophy

by Rick Vaughn

WHEN YOU HUNT DEER ON PUBLIC LAND, you need every edge you can get. If that public land happens to be out-of-state, you face an even greater challenge. But, suppose you also have to abandon your hunting site at the last minute and are forced to still-hunt an unfamiliar tract of land, with an open-sighted muzzleloader in 90-degree heat. For that kind of situation, you'd better have a secret weapon — like an 11-year-old boy.

My son, Clint, and I weren't thinking about the odds when it all began. No, we had something else on our minds back then. That something else was why

we originally found ourselves creeping through the sandy soil of a South Carolina clearcut, navigating by the dim light that just precedes the rising sun. Occasionally, when we paused, we noted the remarkable amount of deer sign that surrounded us. But, there was no time to study it. We hurried toward a line of timber, weaving back and forth among the flowering dogwood trees and the fallen redbud blossoms. We couldn't pause now. After all, we were turkey hunting.

Ahead of us, we could hear a very vocal gobbler from the direction of Clarks Hill Lake, which forms part of the border between South Carolina and Georgia. That old tom was our main target on this warm April morning, but he wasn't the only target. I also felt this area might hold some good whitetails, and I was hoping to bag a bird while I did my spring

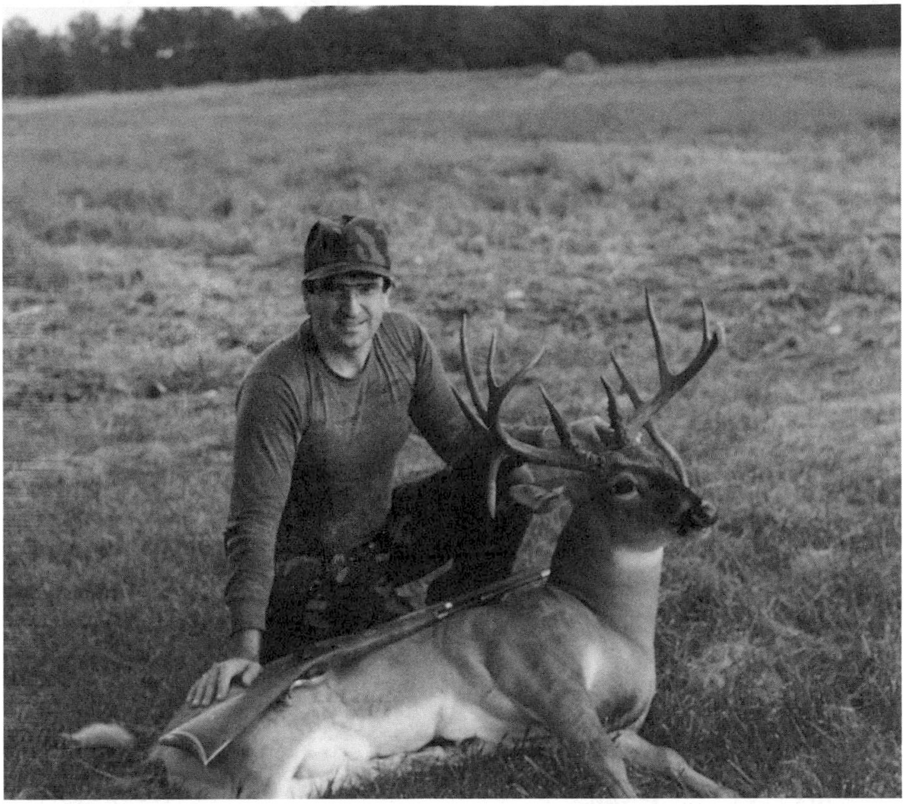

After taking the biggest typical buck of the year in North Carolina, the author fulfilled a personal goal the following season by claiming this trophy — South Carolina's biggest non-typical of 1988. Taken with an open-sighted muzzle-loader, the buck boasted a 24-inch spread and scored 164 3/8 Boone & Crockett points. Photo by Clint Vaughn.

deer scouting. To effectively hunt public-land trophies, I've discovered, scouting needs to be a year-around discipline.

Fortunately, the wandering, all-day-long nature of turkey hunting lends itself very well to this sort of dual purpose. And for many years, I've taken advantage of this time afield to perform both chores. But, this particular day in South Carolina would be different, because I was soon to encounter a most intriguing clue — possibly the most valuable deer secret this region had to offer.

A longtime friend and hunting companion, Steve Vestal, had joined my son and me on this turkey excursion. We'd concentrated our efforts within the general vicinity of the lake and a nearby state park. Steve had a very rewarding day afield and took a nice gobbler, but even more importantly, he discovered a recently dropped antler shed on some publicly hunted game-management property. At the time of our hunt in 1988, this fairly sizable tract was owned by Champion Paper Company, which was the largest private participant in the Wildlife Management Areas program administered by the state.

With five well-balanced points and good mass, the shed antler was quite respectable, especially considering that South Carolina isn't particularly noted for big bucks. As we dined on freshly caught crappies that night and passed the shed around the campfire, each hunter's eyes seemed to gleam. And while we speculated about the size and whereabouts of the shed's owner, we suddenly found ourselves planning next fall's hunt. Sheds are about the most exciting evidence a hunter can find, and this one had truly captured our imaginations.

For trophy hunters, no clue is more descriptive than a shed antler. In fact, searching for late-winter sheds may be the most valuable scouting activity you can perform. Not only does it provide you with an exact "snapshot" of the buck, but you'll have plenty of time before the next season to monitor the deer and plan your strategy.

I had chosen this area because I believed it held the potential for more than just turkeys. Steve's discovery confirmed my suspicions, and likewise proved that some of these deer were successfully evading the local hunting pressure. When I had hunted other states in the past, I sometimes discovered similar isolated pockets of protected whitetails. Each time, the mature bucks were taking advantage of an umbrella of protection formed by a nearby sanctuary. In this case, that sanctuary came in the form of the state park, where no hunting was allowed. Just outside the park were vast cutovers. Their mix of planted pine trees — ranging from a height of 20 feet all the way down to freshly plowed rows of seedlings — supplied the deer with tender new growth as well as cover. The occasional stands of big trees afforded the deer some protection from the crowds of hunters that are so commonplace in this region.

The next couple days were spent analyzing the vicinity where Steve had found the dropped antler. As we extended our search circles outward from the spot, I encountered some old rut sign from an even more impressive "prospect." He had left massive rubs, not to mention scrapes as big as car hoods. They were all linked to an obvious trail that exited one of the tall cutovers on the game land and led straight into the adjacent park. I now had all the information I needed to begin planning an out-of-state deer trip for the fall.

Thanks to my turkey hunting trip, I'd found an ideal sanctuary surrounded by huntable public land. In order to have a reasonable chance to find and hunt big bucks, I look for situations that are conducive to producing mature deer — in other words, places where a buck can stay alive long enough to achieve trophy status. If the hunting pressure and the terrain don't allow a deer to reach maturity (4 1/2 to 8 1/2 years of age), there is little potential for trophy animals there. But once you find a location with such potential and you can verify older bucks are indeed there, your odds of taking a mature trophy buck are greatly enhanced. In this case, the large, varying-age clearcuts adjacent to the state park provided everything the deer needed, including enough cover and protection to reach a ripe old age. I decided to concentrate my hunting efforts within very close proximity of this sheltered buffer zone.

To locate big bucks, hunters should concentrate on areas that provide deer with an opportunity to survive long enough to reach maturity. These "sanctuaries," however small, offer valuable cover that help whitetails escape danger. As long as such havens are present, even heavily hunted areas will have the potential to produce mature trophy bucks.

All through that summer, Clint kept asking me about going back to South Carolina and hunting those bucks we'd found. It reminded me that one of the most enjoyable aspects of hunting is the excitement and anticipation a father and son can share as they wait for fall to arrive. Clint was 11 years old at the time and anxiously awaiting his first out-of-state deer hunt. He had, however, accompanied me on many in-state whitetail hunts near our home in North Carolina, beginning when he was just four years old. He actually started hunting at age nine, taking two bucks that year with his 6mm Rem. While he already had four bucks to his credit, this trip would mark his first attempt at taking a buck with a muzzleloader.

Steve Vestal was unable to join us on opening weekend, so just Clint and I embarked on the trip south to Clarks Hill. At the time, I was concerned that even a little hunting pressure might push the deer back

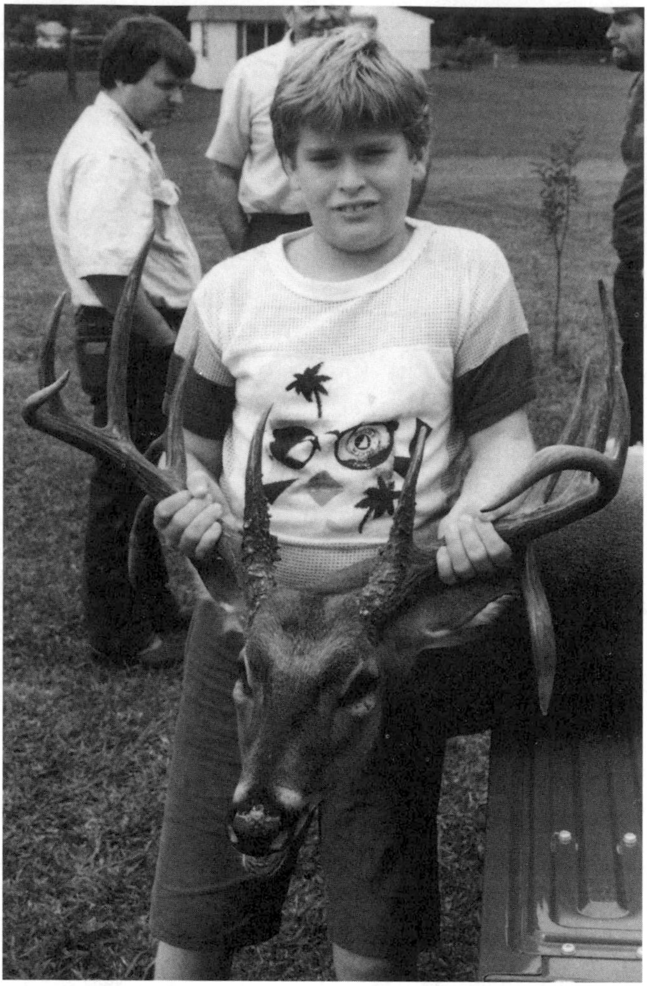
It was Clint Vaughn, the author's 11-year-old son, who first spotted the giant whitetail. Though young, Clint was no novice; he already had taken four bucks of his own in North Carolina! Photo by Rick Vaughn.

across the line and into the shelter of the park. Therefore, we decided to waste no time trying to find the largest buck. That meant being in the woods on opening morning of the state's blackpowder season. We'd be hunting in the Western Piedmont Hunt Unit, which is the name for the zone that encompasses the lake and its surroundings.

Back in the early 1970s, South Carolina was the first state adjacent to my home state of North Carolina to offer a season for blackpowder hunters. I began hunting there in 1975, and over the last 20 years, I've taken many bucks during this early season. The weather is generally mild, and the leaves are just beginning to reflect a multitude of beautiful fall colors. Also, the state allowed hunters under the age of 16 to hunt for free, provided they were accompanied by an adult. It looked like a great opportunity for a father-son hunt.

Opening day in the western Piedmont is October 1, which is looked upon almost as a holiday in the rural stretches of the state. The first-day turnout is always heavy, even though they have a long season and, at the time, a total yearly bag limit of 15 deer. Four-wheel-drive vehicles, with portable tree stands stashed in the back, can be seen on almost every dirt road with public access. Considering all the furor and the resulting hunting pressure, it's easy to see why hunters can have difficulty finding a mature buck on public game lands.

At the start of the season the bucks are relaxed, still banded together and following their summer feeding patterns. However, when such extreme hunting pressure is applied, it doesn't take long for them to retreat to the thickets or other isolated sanctuaries. It's no surprise that over the years in South Carolina I've claimed some of my best bucks on opening day. But, no opener would be more memorable than Saturday, October 1, 1988.

It's a 4 1/2-hour drive from our home in North Carolina to the campsite we had selected near the town of McCormick, and I was amazed to discover how many questions an 11-year-old boy could squeeze into that many hours of riding. Clint's excitement seemed to grow by the mile, and I was experiencing more than my fair share of anticipation as well. That night, we talked for a long time after going to bed. Ever since the early days of my hunting youth, sleep has always been hard to come by on the eve of deer season. By the looks of it, Clint was afflicted with the same malady.

When we emerged from our tent and stepped into the pre-dawn darkness on opening morning, it was already warm and humid. Loading up our well-weathered green Land Cruiser, we were soon bouncing along the old country road, heading for our chosen stand sites. I had planned for us to hunt at the edge of the mature timber, where it intersected a three-year-old cutover.

But, the best-laid plans of mice, men and deer hunters sometimes go astray. As our headlights bounced along the darkened road, we suddenly saw something that caused our hearts to sink. After months of preparation and anticipation, our plans had suddenly come apart at the seams. Though it was more than an hour and a half until daylight, two other hunters had already parked at our spot and were preparing to head into the shadowy woods. Apparently they, too, had scouted the area and come to the same conclusion I had last spring. I walked up to them and exchanged greetings. "Fellows," I said, " you got here first, so we'll hunt elsewhere. Good luck to you!"

It was hard to hide our disappointment, but we quickly considered our options and decided to move to the other side of the clearcut, about three-quarters of a mile away.

Clint was carrying a .45-caliber Seneca made by Thompson/Center Arms. I positioned his portable treestand along a road bed that, judging by the tracks, was heavily travelled by the local deer population. About 200 yards from my son's position, I used my portable climber to ascend a pine that was situated along a line of mature trees. My firearm was one of my old-time favorites, a Browning "mountain rifle" barreled in the popular .50 caliber.

The sun seemed to rise slowly through the thick fog and haze that day. It may have felt longer than it really was, because we spent four uneventful hours perched among the pines. It was very quiet and peaceful, except for the occasional muffled boom of blackpowder guns in the distance. When we eventually made our way back to the vehicle, Clint asked, "Dad, I thought you said the bucks would be in this part of the clearcut. All I saw was a fellow that walked past just at daylight and a few birds!"

By actively hunting throughout the full span of daylight hours, hunters can greatly increase their odds of success. After all, you can't shoot a deer if you're not even in the field. Plus, when other hunters quit or move during midday, they may create opportunities for those who remain.

I was still trying to formulate a new game plan, but I didn't want my son to lose his enthusiasm. "Yeah, I know Clint," I answered, with as much excitement as possible, "but wait until you see the place I have picked out for us to hunt this afternoon."

Glancing down at my watch, I could see that it was 11 o'clock. Already, the humidity was building and the temperature was approaching 90 degrees. Even though it's deer season, October can still pack some sizzling heat in the Palmetto State. Fortunately, due to the heat and the fact that it was nearly lunchtime, this back side of the clearcut seemed devoid of hunters.

We drove down a logging road until I found a reason to pull over and park. There, near the edge of the cutover, was a windrow. Sometimes left behind after timber is harvested, these windrows consist of bulldozed limbs, roots and stumps. Blackberries, honeysuckle, polkberries, tender grasses, vines and other new growth sprout up vigorously from the loose,

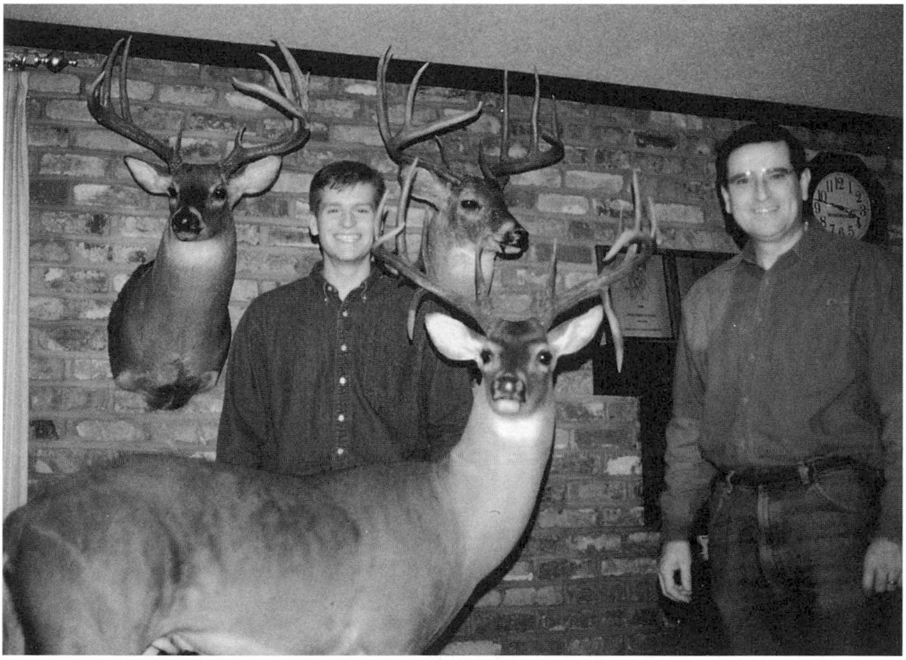

Six years after their memorable hunt, Clint (left) and his father pose with the full-bodied mount of the trophy buck. At the 1989 Dixie Deer Classic in Raleigh, North Carolina, the deer was honored as the top non-typical of the year from South Carolina. Photo by Anthony Avant.

rich soil that remains among the rotting tree roots. I knew that windrows not only provided excellent food for deer, but that whitetails also liked to bed in their vicinity. These windrows might also be appealing, I thought, because they offered a good vantage point for the deer to watch any activity within the cut.

Clint and I were engaging in one of the best "in-season" scouting techniques I know for hunters. Short excursions within clearcuts are a great way to investigate deer activity in the area, and they also clue you in to the presence of other hunters. Sometimes, if you move slowly and carefully along the windrows, a buck will bound out of a hiding spot, run a short distance and then stop to take a look back at whatever it was that disturbed him. We were now in the clearcut that adjoined the state park, and I decided we'd try to find the best locations to place our stands for that afternoon's hunt. Also, by electing to stay afield the entire day, we were trying to prevent a repeat of our disappointing experience in the morning, when we were beaten to our preferred location. Despite our change in plans and the oppressive heat, I was determined to do everything I could to salvage the day.

As is so often the case in life — and especially when hunting whitetails — the moment of opportunity came when we least expected it. As we steadily crept along the windrow, Clint suddenly turned toward me. "Dad," he whispered, "there's a buck, but he's too far for me to shoot."

My son had been alertly checking our back trail when he caught a glimpse of a huge buck. The deer was staring at us calmly, standing perfectly motionless as he watched us walk past. Moving like molasses in winter, I slowly eased a percussion cap onto the nipple and gently raised the muzzleloader to my shoulder.

Peering down the barrel through the old-fashioned iron sights, I carefully engaged the set trigger. While aiming, I wondered what the deer was thinking as he continued to study us with such an intent gaze. Because South Carolina didn't allow scopes on muzzleloaders, I couldn't make out all the details of the buck's rack. That was probably in my favor; otherwise, I might have had trouble holding the gun steady. I carefully squeezed the trigger. As the smoke billowed from the gun's barrel, I could see the buck stumble and lumber off.

We counted 147 paces to where the buck had been standing. There, we quickly found scattered blood spoor that indicated a lung shot. After following the trail for just 100 yards, we found the deer, already dead.

He was a magnificent monarch, much more impressive than I had thought. The huge buck carried a rack 24 inches wide that featured 10 typical points, two non-typical drop tines and an abnormal point growing off the G-2 on his right beam. He also carried 227 pounds of body weight beneath those antlers, which is exceptionally heavy for a Carolina whitetail.

Hunting trips with youngsters can be rewarding in many different ways. Success can be especially sweet when it's shared with a son or daughter, but you don't have to take a trophy to create some special memories that last a lifetime.

It was truly an unforgettable hunting experience, especially since it was shared with my favorite hunting partner — my son. If it had not been for his hunting instincts and alert eyes, I may have never seen the buck. Understandably, I was a pretty proud father, and thankful for the opportunity we had received that day.

Not long after we had placed the buck on the old Land Cruiser and started home, two men passed by with amazed looks on their faces. Yes, they were the same hunters who had arrived at the cutover ahead of us that morning. "You know, Clint," I said, "the early bird doesn't always get the worm. And, you remember another story about the tortoise and hare? Well, who ends up in first place?"

Soon after, I had a full-body mount made of the deer. Though I have 20 or so deer mounts, including some bucks with even higher net scores, this one was special. From beginning to end, it was a team effort. Later, when the North Carolina muzzleloading season opened, I made sure Clint was on one of my favorite stands. This time it was his turn to shine. After passing up a 4-pointer and an 8-pointer, he tagged a beautiful 20-inch 9-pointer.

One day, after the taxidermy work was complete, Clint and I were reflecting on all the circumstances that led us to the huge buck in South Carolina. While sitting in our den, I said, "Clint, without you, I would have probably never seen our 'Carolina Dandy.' In appreciation for your help, I've decided to give you that .270 Winchester pre-64 Model 70 you've always liked. It's a great old rifle, and one that I want you to keep to give to your son one day.

"I might even part with another rare old Winchester," I added, "if you could possibly locate another wallhanger for a rapidly aging old man like me to shoot!" He just smiled and slowly shook his head.

The 6x7 non-typical scored a net 164 3/8 Boone & Crockett points. When I later entered it in the 1989 Dixie Deer Classic, it won its category as the best deer taken in South Carolina that year. That allowed me to win back-to-back North and South Carolina Deer Classic honors, as I had won the North Carolina award for the state's best typical deer (scoring 158 7/8) the previous year.

That was a goal I had set out to accomplish several seasons earlier. Thanks to my favorite hunting partner, it finally became a reality.

Chapter Eleven

Hunting The Invisible Buck

by Greg Miller

If only I could move!

After sitting rock-still for so long, my muscles were beginning to rebel, aching and shivering in the sub-zero cold. But I didn't dare budge, or even take a deep breath. Not now. Not yet.

Just 20 yards in front of me, six mature does were busily pawing through the three inches of crusty snow blanketing the ground. The deer had cautiously made their way into the open field just five minutes earlier, after the skittish does finally seemed confident enough to leave the woods. Once they left their shelter, the deer quickly became absorbed in uncovering some of the unharvested alfalfa that lay beneath the snow. As they picked their way though the field, they drifted closer and closer to my perch in the old oak tree. They were within bow range now, but they were in no danger. I wasn't after them. I was waiting for another rendezvous, with an old nemesis I had never seen.

Fighting off the cold, I sat motionless as the does continued to mill around in front of me. Then, faintly at first, I heard some ever-so-soft crunching sounds coming from the wooded bluff on my left. After listening to the approaching footsteps for some time, I slowly turned my head to take a look. It must be another doe or fawn, I thought, coming to join the

After almost two years of scouting and hunting a buck he had never seen, the author took his trophy on a frigid, sub-zero December afternoon. The buck was the biggest non-typical bowkill of the year in Wisconsin. Photo by Jeff Miller.

others. Not so! What I saw kicked my heart into hyperdrive.

Just 30 yards away and walking straight toward me was not another doe, but one of the biggest whitetail bucks I'd ever seen! His massive antlers towered high above his head, and the inside spread of his beams was far greater than the width of his ears. He was the buck I'd been waiting for, and he was huge. Best of all, if he just stayed on his current path, the monster whitetail was going to pass within 15 yards of my stand site. In the next few seconds — if everything went exactly right — I'd finally get my chance at the trophy of a lifetime.

It had been a long, frustrating wait. That's because my pursuit of this mysterious giant actually had started nearly two years earlier in the spring of 1989 when my brother, Jeff, and I gained access to a 290-acre tract of private farmland near our homes in west-central Wisconsin. On our very first spring scouting trip to the farm, we uncovered enough clues to convince us that at least one tremendous buck lived in the immediate vicinity. Brimming with enthusiasm, we spent an enormous amount of time learning all we could about the terrain we'd be hunting. By the time our preseason scouting came to a conclusion, we were ready. We felt sure we'd get a crack at the monster buck during the archery season.

But, the 1989 bowhunting season came and went without incident. Oh, we saw plenty of deer on the farm, including a couple of dandy bucks. But Jeff and I both believed that neither of those animals could have been responsible for the huge, distinctive rubs that had appeared almost daily during the season. And certainly, none of the bucks we'd seen so far had made the enormous hoof prints we'd spotted in certain areas of the farm.

To be honest, I didn't spend a great deal of time hunting the farm that season. Some hunters may wonder (and rightfully so) why I didn't dedicate more time to a deer that showed every indication of being a trophy. But at the time, my heart still belonged to the big woods. For the past 20 years, I'd spent nearly all of my hunting time in the forests of northern Wisconsin. To say that I was intrigued with woodland whitetails would have been a vast understatement. As far as I'm concerned, those deer are perhaps the ultimate challenge for a modern-day trophy hunter.

It's possible to identify individual bucks purely by their rubs. For instance, scratches or gouges in "odd" places on rubbed trees can indicate the presence of a buck with non-typical or sticker points on his rack. By examining rubs carefully and watching for telltale similarities, you can eliminate a lot of the mystery concerning which deer made which rubs.

Also, many of the big woods bucks I was hunting at the time were leaving behind sign just as impressive as what we'd seen on the farm. From my perspective, it made no sense to turn my back on several huge deer on tracts that I knew intimately in order to go hunt another buck that might be no bigger and lived in an area I'd never hunted. Consequently, the farmland buck took a back seat to his more familiar cousins that year.

Nonetheless, Jeff and I spent a great deal of time scouting the farm before the 1990 archery season. Even though we found a fair amount of buck sign, it didn't appear that the big deer was spending much time on our acreage. He left behind only a few of his unique calling cards — the huge, oddly-shaped gouges in his rub trees that we'd seen last year. (The

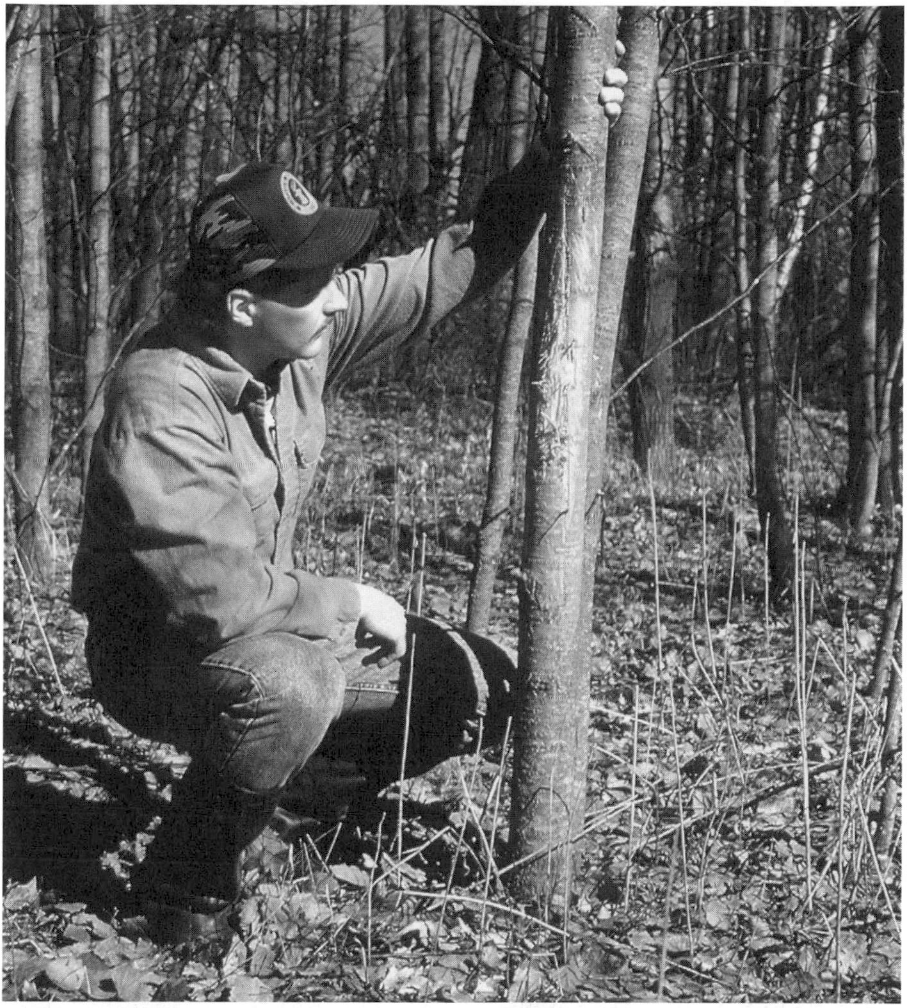

Because the big buck left distinctive rubs, caused by one of his non-typical points, the author was able to tell which rubs had been made by "his" deer. As a result, he was able to locate specific rub lines and search for places where those lines intersected. That's where he hunted. Photo by Greg Miller.

unusual shape and nature of the markings had led us to believe the buck might be at least slightly non-typical.) Apparently, he was an occasional visitor instead of a resident on the farm.

Figuring out how to hunt the big buck was becoming a frustrating endeavor. The farm had plenty of open ground, and we were able to keep an eye on most of the land when we hunted. But even though Jeff and I had been chasing this buck off and on for nearly two full seasons now, we were still waiting for our first glimpse of the trophy animal. Although he was apparently very active after dark, each morning before daylight the buck would tuck himself away in some inaccessible sanctuary. We weren't surprised by his reclusive behavior, however. We've come to expect it from mature bucks of his class.

There had been one time in December 1989 when Jeff thought he might have seen "our" buck. My brother was watching from a distance one day, simply observing late-afternoon deer activity on the farm. Just as daylight was beginning to fade, a huge buck walked out into the open about 400 yards away. "It really was too far and too dark for me to be sure just exactly what he had for points," Jeff told me. "All I know is that even at that distance he looked to be really big."

I was becoming convinced the big buck was almost totally nocturnal and obsessively shy. But, a short time before the 1990 season opened, I learned about a critical aspect of the deer's behavior.

It was apparent from our scouting that when he did visit our farm, the buck preferred one particular part of the acreage over all others. That spot was where a fairly wide brushline extended perhaps 100 yards out from a good-sized wooded bluff. The brushline, which separated a large alfalfa field from a smaller CRP field, fell about 20 yards short of connecting with a small, dense woodlot. Our scouting trips revealed that the big buck had established three different rub lines, all leading into the same corner where the brushline met the wooded bluff. Even more interesting, a great deal of rubs and scrapes seemed to be concentrated near one large, gnarly red oak. That oak was situated on the brushline perhaps 50 yards from the bluff. Intriguingly, the giant buck Jeff had seen the previous December had walked directly beneath this same oak tree when it entered the alfalfa field. Needless to say, I took some time during that off-season to prepare the oak for one of my portable tree stands.

Even though a big whitetail buck may use a lot of different travel corridors when moving through his range, there usually are a couple of routes he'll use more often than others. Of course, these routes will show far more rub/scrape activity than the others. Keep scouting until you feel confident you've located a deer's primary travel routes.

Armed with these new revelations, I decided to get serious about hunting the farmland buck during the 1990 season. Because fresh rub lines enabled us to pinpoint the exact location of the deer's travel routes, I spent most of my time hunting from strategically placed portable tree stands along those trails. In addition to my frequent hunts on the farm, I also did a fair amount of in-season scouting. As you might suspect, I paid close attention to the brushline and especially the area around the old oak. If the big buck revisited his favorite part of the farm, I wanted to know immediately.

There's certainly nothing wrong with dedicating most (or all) of your hunting time to one particular buck. However, that time should be divided among many different stand sites scattered across the buck's home range. Don't get into the habit of devoting all your attention to only one or two stands.

But that area, which had shown so much rub and scrape activity the past two years, never came to life. There was no evidence of any deer working the location on a regular basis. Although I did sit in the old oak on a couple of occasions during the late pre-rut, it was more a stab in the dark than anything else. By the time Wisconsin's early archery season ended, Jeff and I were more frustrated than ever. It appeared that our super-secretive big buck, which was still unseen, would once again evade our efforts.

A few weeks later in early December, I was catching up on some writing assignments at home when Jeff stopped in. He had taken a big 10-pointer during our nine-day gun season in November, and our conversation soon turned to whitetails.

During the season, many hunters believe that every minute of their spare time should be spent hunting, but you should also continue to scout. You never know when new factors might change a deer's behavior or when in-season scouting may provide you with that last clue you need to harvest the buck of a lifetime.

"I was down at the farm this morning doing a bit of looking around," Jeff told me. "I'd hate to guess how many deer are using our alfalfa field as their main source of food right now. There are runways coming into the field from every direction. The deer really have things torn up, the way they're pawing through the snow trying to get at that alfalfa. "Oh, by the way," he added, almost as an afterthought, "I noticed that big buck has got a lot of large trees torn up right around your

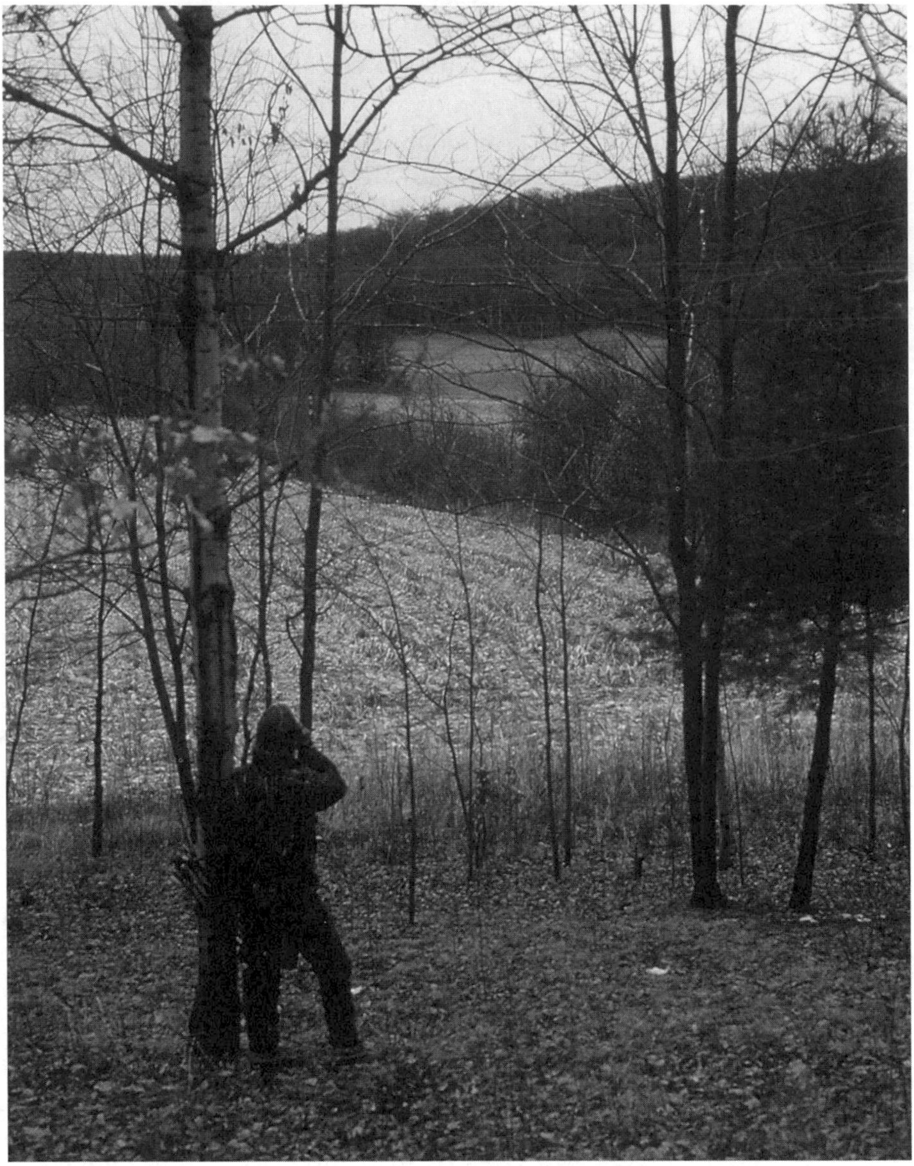

Despite being scouted almost year-around, the super shy whitetail continually eluded the two brothers. The deer's activity was almost completely nocturnal, rendering him virtually invisible and almost impossible to hunt. Finally, on a cold December day, he slipped up. Photo by Greg Miller.

stand on the fence line, doesn't he?"

I stared hard at my brother for a second. "There were only a few big rubs near that stand when I hunted there during the pre-rut," I replied.

My earlier trips, I explained to Jeff, hadn't provided me with any real evidence the big buck had been spending time on the farm — at least not that part of the farm.

"Well, he's there now," Jeff quickly replied. "I noticed a bunch of fresh rubs on big trees along the fence line. And, I found quite a few huge hoof prints in the snow, well within bow range of the oak your stand is in. I'd say he's using the alfalfa as his prime food source right now. If you get some time, I think it might be a good idea for you to sit on that stand one afternoon just to see what's happening."

Like most serious whitetail hunters, I normally don't need much of an excuse to go hunting, especially when a big deer is involved. But along with having several writing deadlines to meet, I was hesitant because hunting conditions had been extremely poor during our late archery season. We had been experiencing temperatures well above normal for December, and this unusually warm weather had disrupted the movements of deer on our farm. In fact, our most recent observations showed us that even the antlerless deer weren't showing up to feed in the alfalfa field until the last light of day. So, I doubted seriously if "Mr. Wonderful" would make an appearance in legal shooting time. What I desperately needed, I realized, was a drastic change of weather.

It's always important — but especially late in the season — to pay close attention to any change in existing weather patterns. A sudden cold snap or an approaching storm front can sometimes trigger a whitetail feeding frenzy or an increase in rutting activity.

Throughout the next few days, I worked feverishly to get caught up on my writing. I also paid very close attention to the weather reports. Finally, on the evening of December 12, I heard the news I'd been waiting for. Weather forecasters were calling for strong northwest winds and rapidly falling temperatures during the late afternoon hours of the next day. In addition, they were predicting a major winter storm with significant accumulations of snow would be moving into the area later the following night. Finally, it appeared that conditions would be perfect for a post-rut hunt.

The forecast for December 13 was right on the money. Temperatures were relatively mild throughout the morning hours, hovering around the freezing mark. But about noon, the winds switched to the northwest and picked up in intensity. At that point, the temperature went into a nose dive. By the time I left the house at two o'clock that afternoon to go hunting, the temperature was a very chilly 15 degrees and still dropping.

By 2:45, I had settled into my stand in the oak tree. For awhile, I thought my clothing scheme was more than adequate to deal with the cold. But a fairly strong wind, carrying colder temperatures with it, quickly pushed the thermometer below the zero mark. I hunkered deeper into my outer layer of clothes and tried to concentrate on something other than the cold. In a few minutes, my mind was occupied with memories of other hunts. It wasn't long before I had completely forgotten about the temperature.

An hour later, as the sun approached the horizon, the wind mercifully died down to little more than a breeze. That, coupled with the sound of a deer walking through the frozen, crusty snow, instantly elevated my body temperature. I stood up slowly, grabbed my bow, and attempted to spot the animal that was working its way toward my position. After only a few seconds, I spotted the deer. It was a buck fawn, and he was on a course that would take him directly under my tree.

Without hesitating, the little deer continued on until he was a mere five yards behind me. Suddenly, he slammed to a stop, stuck his nose straight up in the air and tested the wind. After several seconds of alternately sniffing and looking, the fawn spun around and ran back the way he had come. When he was perhaps 100 yards away, he stopped, looked in my direction and snorted five or six times. "Great," I thought to myself. "That should keep any other deer from coming out to feed this afternoon!"

Too many times, a lack of concentration costs bowhunters a chance at a big whitetail. In most cases, these hunters spend too much time staring at antlers and not enough time concentrating on the spot where they want their arrow to hit. Make sure you focus your attention on the shot, not those big antlers.

But my concern over the buck's behavior was short-lived. The sound of his final snort had barely faded away when I heard more deer working their way toward me from the wooded bluff to my left. I turned my attention in that direction, and it wasn't long before those six does slipped out of the cover and eased their way into the alfalfa field to begin feeding. Ten minutes later, when I heard his footsteps, I turned and saw the monster buck for

Long beams, great mass and huge brow tines allowed the author's big non-typical to easily make the Pope and Young record book with a net score of 193 7/8. The trophy whitetail, which sported 18 scorable points, barely failed to reach the 195 score needed to qualify for the Boone and Crockett book. Photo by Jeff Miller.

the first time.

I felt my knees begin to shake as soon as I set eyes on him. Instinctively, my left hand reached out to grab my bow off its hanger, but as soon as it did, the does spooked and darted away from me. I froze and held my breath. Behind me, the big buck suddenly stopped and, with head high and ears pinned back, watched the retreating does. "That's it," I thought. "He's going to run back into the woods." But he didn't. After a few tense moments, the buck lowered his head, flicked his tail and continued walking toward me.

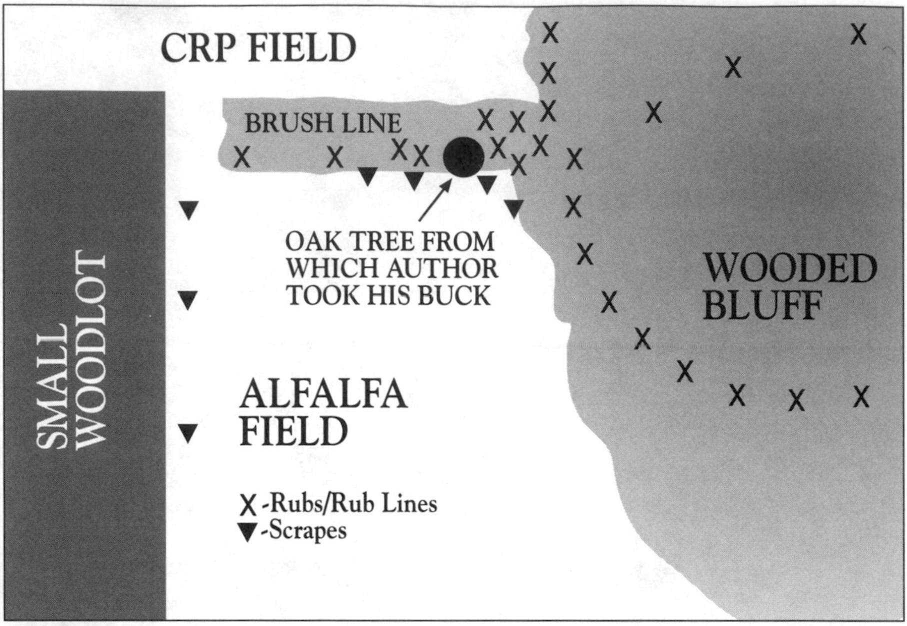

By locating the area where three of the buck's rub lines converged (and where the deer also had made several scrapes), the author was able to find some promising sites for portable tree stands. He finally took the huge whitetail while hunting from a red oak tree that was situated in a brushline adjacent to an alfalfa field. The buck emerged late in the day from the wooded bluff.

He was just 20 yards away now. In an attempt to regain my composure, I bit down lightly on my bottom lip and concentrated on the buck's kill zone. With just a few more steps, he would offer me a perfect broadside shot. At that point, I'd draw my bow, put the 20-yard sight pin in the center of his lung area and make a smooth release. It had all the earmarks of a perfect setup.

And then, the buck did one of those unpredictable things that make mature whitetails so difficult to hunt. Just as I was starting to draw, he abruptly turned and faced me head-on. He stopped walking, looked around for a few seconds, then dropped his head and began nibbling on some alfalfa the does had uncovered. Here, I had the buck of a lifetime a mere 15 yards away, and he was standing at an angle that made him impossible to shoot. This was not the way it was supposed to happen!

Time stopped as I waited, frozen in position and scarcely breathing. Every so often, the buck would lift his head, survey his surroundings and then go back to gobbling down more alfalfa. A minute passed, then another, and he was still facing directly toward me. There was no way I'd even consider taking a shot at that angle. Would he ever move? To keep my heart from beating any faster, I forced myself not to look at his gigantic antlers.

Actually, there was one positive side effect of my quandary. The longer the buck remained in that position, the more convinced I became that he was going to detect my presence eventually and bolt away without ever offering me a shot. This train of thought, while not very comforting, did wonders for my nerves. I was so sure I wasn't going to get a shot at the buck, I actually became quite calm.

I'd been watching the buck for about two minutes before he finally made a slight turn to his right. While the angle had improved some, I still couldn't be sure of delivering a fatal shot. "Come on, big fella," I silently urged. "Turn just a little bit more."

As if hearing my plea, the monster buck moved even more to his right. He still wasn't quite broadside, but I knew this angle would allow me to make a clean shot. Now I had to actually make that shot.

Coming to full draw, I centered my sight pin on the point of the buck's nearest shoulder. I held for a few seconds, double-checked the sight picture and released my arrow. The Zwickey-tipped shaft hit exactly where I was aiming. Instantly, the buck was off and running. His first few bounds carried him back toward the bluff. But then, he noticed that the does were running full-tilt across the alfalfa field. He changed his course and fell in behind the caravan of escaping deer.

I watched from my stand as the big deer galloped 100 yards out into the field. "He should tip over any second now," I said to myself. But, the buck pressed on. At 200 yards, the does made a quick left turn. The buck did likewise. I started having doubts about the severity of the hit.

Suddenly, the does made another sharp left turn. The buck, however, continued straight ahead. After several more bounds, he went down in a shower of snow. I watched him through my binoculars to see if he was going to get up, but the big deer was down for good.

Although I told myself I should take my time and approach the downed buck with caution, I'm sure I covered the 200-plus yards in world-class time. As I approached him, I realized the buck was even bigger than I had first thought. I knelt down next to him, grabbed one of his massive antlers and lifted his head out of the snow. I marveled at the huge rack for about a half minute before gently laying the buck's head back down.

The next 10 minutes were an emotional time. I talked to myself and to the buck. I stood in complete silence for several minutes and just admired him. There were tears of both joy and sorrow. Yes, I was extremely happy that my two-year quest for the buck had finally come to a successful end. But on the other hand, I had to admit to a certain degree of sadness. This magnificent creature laying before me would no longer be roaming the farm, leaving behind tantalizing sign that made me feel like I knew him. I realized that my future hunts on the farm would never be quite the same.

Jeff showed up just in time to shoot a few photos of the buck before it was totally dark. Then we loaded him into the back of my brother's truck and headed off across the field.

"I know we've got the big buck in the back of my truck," said Jeff as we pulled up to the landowner's house, "but I still can't believe he's dead. It just doesn't seem real."

I turned and looked at the monster deer on the tailgate. "I know what you mean," I replied. "This whole ordeal seems like a dream."

After the required 60-day drying period, Craig Cousins, an official scorer, measured the antlers of my late-season trophy. The gross score was 202 5/8 non-typical, with a final net score of 193 7/8. The buck was the biggest archery non-typical taken in Wisconsin that season. And at the time he was measured, he ranked as the fourth largest non-typical bowkill ever recorded in the state.

The buck's rack has a basic 10-point frame that nets 165 5/8 as a typical, with eight more non-typical points totaling 28 2/8 inches. The inside spread is 21 1/8 inches, while the main beams are 27 6/8 and 26 3/8 inches in length. The circumference measurements on the antlers add up to an impressive 42 2/8 inches! The deer, which appeared old and gaunt, was judged to be at least 7 1/2 years old.

But even had the buck been far less endowed in the antler department, he still would have been a great trophy in my eyes. The way I see it, anytime a whitetail buck is able to evade your every move for nearly two years and never allows you to see him even once during that time, he certainly has achieved trophy status.

In the end, I believe I was able to take the buck not so much because of what I did right, but because of the things the deer did wrong. He first endangered himself when he left his bedding sanctuary much earlier than normal. Then, his appetite led him away from the wooded bluff and into an open field in broad daylight. And on that one day when he made his mistakes, I just happened to be waiting in the right spot.

CHAPTER TWELVE

In Search Of A Texas Trophy

by Bob Zaiglin

IS THERE ANY GREATER CHALLENGE than pursuing a world-class whitetail?

Before you answer, consider these odds. Each season in America, 11 million whitetail hunters spend over 113 million days in the field, many searching for that buck of a lifetime. In a good year, those hunters will take perhaps 400 whitetails that qualify for the Boone and Crockett record book. That's about one "book" deer for every 27,000 hunters, or one for every 282,000 hunting days.

You can, of course, try a few things that might improve your odds. For example, you could spend your entire life hunting and studying deer, and maybe even earn a master's degree in range and wildlife management. Then, you could take a job as the wildlife manager for a fabled 100,000-acre ranch in South Texas, overseeing a trophy-rich deer population where hunting is carefully controlled.

Yes, you can do all of those things — like I did — and still spend years and years — like I did — trying to take the buck of your dreams. It's not supposed to be easy, even in the semiarid Brush Country of Texas where trophy bucks are legendary.

Growing up in the Pennsylvania hardwoods, where hunting pressure made big deer a rarity, I could only dream of matching wits with a record-class buck. But once I moved to Texas and went to work at Harrison Ranches, I realized that such a possibility really did exist. Even so, I was

Almost a year from when he first spotted the deer, the author finally beat the odds and claimed this great South Texas trophy. The beautifully symmetrical rack notched a net score of 171 3/8, earning it a spot in the Boone and Crockett record book. Photo courtesy of Bob Zaiglin.

hardly prepared for the day when I finally came face-to-face with my fantasy.

Because I work on three large ranches separated by many miles, I don't have a lot of time to hunt on my own. But occasionally, I do some guiding for the ranch owners, and on this particular January morning in 1993, I was helping Bruce Harrison try to locate a big non-typical I'd spotted earlier in the season.

We had positioned ourselves near a crossroads where the non-typical had been seen before. It was a miserable morning, cold and damp, and at first we saw nothing. But as morning's light began to stubbornly seep through the gray, overcast skies, the Brush Country came to life. What we saw was unreal. Bucks of all sizes seemed to pour out of the brush, crossing back and forth all around us. But we didn't see the non-typical, or any other truly trophy-sized bucks ... at least not at first.

Then, suddenly, a slight movement in the distance caught my eye. I

The low-growing brush that dominates the terrain of South Texas serves the deer population in two important ways. First, it provides ideal cover in the semiarid landscape. Secondly, it offers highly nutritious forage that helps produce some of the finest bucks in North America. Photo by Bob Zaiglin.

swallowed hard as I stared at a buck that had materialized before us. It was a 12-pointer, a monstrous deer, with perfectly matched tines that stretched upward like a picket fence. Without a doubt, he was a 170-class typical buck — the kind of deer that many hunters spend their lives trying to find. But before any attempt at a shot could be made, he vanished into the sea of brush.

I was stunned. Now that he had disappeared, the incident seemed almost unreal. Had he really been that big? And just as important, would I ever see him again?

I searched for the rest of that season but never caught another glimpse of the deer. Still, the vision of him continued to haunt my thoughts. The following spring, I trudged mile after mile through the thorny brush, searching for the shed antlers of the 12-pointer or the non-typical. Without recovering those cast antlers, I had no way to be sure that either deer had survived the winter, or their exact size. I kept scanning the dry, red soil for their fallen antlers, but they were nowhere to be found.

High-scoring bucks are basically freaks of nature. They are rare even on the best of ranches, and hunting true trophy bucks is always a gamble. While it's not difficult to take a buck in South Texas, top-end trophies are another matter, considering that these deer represent the top two or three percent of all the bucks in a population.

For the next several months, I could only speculate about the survival and possible whereabouts of the giant bucks. But a bit of luck early that fall revived my hopes.

Someone on the ranch reported seeing the non-typical about two miles north of the crossroads where he (and the 12-pointer) had been seen during the January rut. To me, that meant that the deer's summer core area was two miles north of his favored breeding ground. That explained why I hadn't found his shed antlers; he'd probably moved out of the crossroads area after the rut. I'd simply been searching the wrong place. The discovery also reinforced my theory that you should scout for big bucks during the hunting season, because at other times of the year they may be in a different location.

In South Texas, the rut occurs during the hunting season. That means that your best time for scouting next year's buck is while you are hunting this year's animal. Based on my observations and other research, bucks return to the same breeding grounds each season.

So, I knew the non-typical was alive, I knew where he was now and I knew where he would be when the rut rolled around again. The 12-pointer, I hoped, would follow the same pattern.

By the time the 1993-94 season arrived, my excitement level was maxed out. Not only did I feel that the 12-pointer would soon be back in his breeding ground, but we'd had back-to-back years of wet springtime weather, which had provided ideal nutrition for antler growth in the deer herd. And because this region of Texas has consistently demonstrated the ability to produce 170-class deer, I knew the conditions were about as good as they would get for such antlers to show up.

On December 3, I met up with my hunting partner and client, David Shashy from Florida. David was the first person ever to hunt this huge ranch with me, and our years of hunting together had created a strong friendship.

Not long after stowing our gear, we were in a high-racked truck, negotiating our way along the red, sandy roads of Dimmit County. At a little over 100,000 acres, we had plenty of room to roam. The ranch is located in the middle of Texas' three best counties for B&C bucks, covering parts of Dimmit, Webb and LaSalle. In addition, it had experienced very little hunting pressure. The doe population is controlled through careful harvest, helping to maintain a tight sex ratio and a healthy herd. The buck hunting is highly selective.

Even during deer season, the weather in South Texas is often hot and sultry, and that's exactly what David and I encountered. Instead of glassing the desert-like expanses from the truck, we elected to concentrate on the water holes, where we felt the deer would seek relief from the heat. It turned out to be a good decision. On the third day of the hunt, David collected his best-ever buck, a dark-beamed trophy we scored as a 168. It was a magnificent deer.

Now that David had a buck, I had an opportunity to do some hunting myself. He stayed on, and we split up to cover more ground. Although a great deal of hunting in Texas is done from high-racked trucks, I prefer to remain stationary and hunt from either a tripod or a box blind. When elevated over the brush, both types of stands provide great visibility. Generally, I set up my blinds around the many oat fields we've planted for the deer. These areas attract does like a magnet, and during the rut, the bucks will never be far from the does. Unlike the lush fields of crops you can find in most parts of the country, those in South Texas receive precious little rain. As a result, most oat patches are blotchy and sparse instead of being carpeted in green. Even without much visible oats, however, the disked patches or strips are still attractive to deer, which use them as travel lanes and to make scrape lines.

I decided to set up 300 yards north of David in a tripod. From my elevated perch, I hoped to locate bucks that were venturing out of their daytime lairs to feed or search for does. Just before sundown during the prime deer movement period, two young bucks appeared in front of me but suddenly darted off. Searching the brush for whatever had spooked them, I was surprised to see David striding toward me along a sendero, one

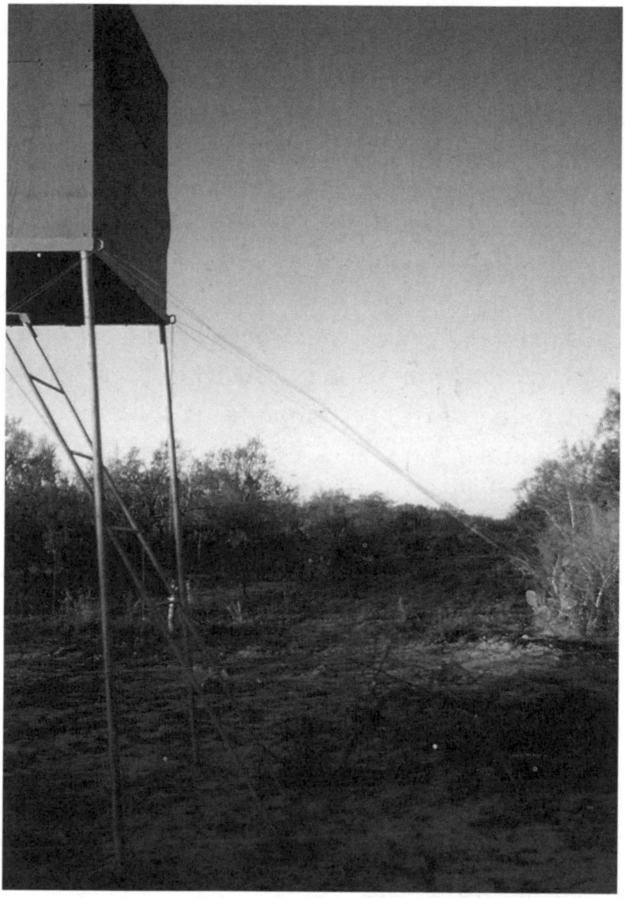

Searching for deer from high-racked trucks is popular in Texas, but the author often prefers to remain stationary in an elevated blind or tripod. He believes the greater visibility offered by such blinds coupled with better concealment of the hunter outweigh the mobility of hunting from a truck, especially when hunting wary top-end bucks. Photo by Bob Zaiglin.

of the long man-made lanes through the brush. What on earth could have compelled an avid deer hunter to abandon his blind during the peak deer-hunting time?

When he reached me, David could hardly contain himself. From the base of my tripod, he excitedly blurted out that he had just seen the biggest deer of his life, a huge 12-pointer.

That evening, all we could think about was the big buck. David even sketched the deer's rack for me on the back of his business card. We discussed what we thought he would score and began formulating our plans for the next day. To try to get a handle on the deer's pattern, I decided to ask Shance Tyson, one of our wildlife interns, to sit in the tripod the next morning and watch for the 12-pointer. David and I would set up in the box blind, which was elevated over a small food plot with several narrow disked strips extending outward from the plot for 100 yards, much like the spokes of a wagon wheel. Dry conditions had killed off the oats, but deer still frequented the area.

From the box blind, David and I saw several nice bucks that morning. But, the 12-pointer never showed. We later found out why. Shance, alone in the tripod, had watched the deer much of the morning as it worked several scrapes within a few yards of him. Our double-teaming efforts were working. Knowing that the deer was staying in the same general area heightened my confidence. I now believed I was going to meet up with the 12-pointer again — I just didn't know when.

But over the next few days, my confidence began to erode. Perched in the tripod beside a large mesquite tree, I spent two days trying to cope with howling north winds. The winds were so strong I had to anchor my seat to the tree to keep from being spun around. As the weather turned cold and the wind shook everything in sight, the deer turned spooky and scarce. I did see several bucks, including a 10-pointer with super-tall tines that may have scored in the mid-160s, but the 12-pointer never showed. David, hunting from the box blind, didn't see him either.

Rattling is an extremely effective way of attracting big bucks to your blind or stand, but it can also backfire. Younger bucks may rush in, become alarmed and wind up spooking the more mature trophy deer that you're actually trying to hunt.

At times, especially when the wind died down, I was tempted to try rattling. But up until that point, the deer had been undisturbed, and I decided to keep it that way. I might be able to lure him in by rattling, but I also might attract some younger naive bucks that would spook and give my position away. No, I'd sit tight and wait.

By December 14, David had departed for home, and I had another hunter due at the ranch. When the hunter called that morning and said he wouldn't be arriving until late in the afternoon, I took advantage of the extra hours and took off in the direction of the tripod. But for some reason, I changed my mind. Call it intuition, reverse psychology or blind luck, but something told me to hunt from the box blind instead.

This day, the winds were calm and the sky was clear. Quietly, I climbed into the blind and began scanning the dried-up oat patch and brush in front of me. Within minutes, I detected a slight movement on a grassy bank that rose up from a mesquite-laden bottom. Through my binoculars, I could see two does. Anxiously, I glassed the area behind them, searching for signs of a buck in pursuit. Nothing. On the horizon, the warm glow of the afternoon sun began to wane into the evening, and

Eight days before the author took his trophy, hunting partner David Shashy claimed his best buck ever by hunting over a water hole on the same ranch. It scored 168 B&C points. Photo by Bob Zaiglin.

the two does slowly disappeared into the tall grass.

As I pulled my eye away from the binoculars, I froze. There, not 40 yards away, was the 12-pointer! He was as awesome as I remembered, and now he was walking toward me, paralleling a disked strip of red Texas soil. He came closer and closer until, just 20 feet from the blind, he stopped and stood motionless behind a big prickly ash bush. It was the last obstruction between me and the trophy buck.

Then, for the longest 15 minutes imaginable to a deer hunter, that deer remained hidden behind the prickly ash. I still hadn't had a good look at his rack, but I could see him working his antlers in the thorny brush. Unlike most South Texas bucks during breeding season, he was unusually calm. But I wasn't. I strained to gain a glimpse of his rack, but I just couldn't see it through the bush. Finally, I moved slightly in the 4-foot-by-6-foot blind and discovered a tiny hole through the bush where I could spy his antlers.

It's easy to tell if a buck has a huge rack, even with the naked eye.

But to score a deer on the hoof, you need good optics. I had two problems at the moment. First, the narrow opening in the bush never allowed me to see both sides of his rack at once, so I couldn't tell how well one side matched the other. Secondly, he was so close that my 10x40 binoculars didn't provide any perspective. I found myself attempting to mentally tape his rack, as if it were in my living room, comparing him to other bucks whose dimensions I knew.

Distinguishing a trophy-sized rack is easy, but to critically analyze the total inches and the scoring potential of antlers, a good set of binoculars is a must. For long-range situations, a spotting scope may well be necessary.

I could tell immediately that he carried a 170-class frame, but my brief glimpses of his antlers suggested that his left side sported a short G-2 tine, perhaps two inches shorter than the one on the right beam. I knew from experience that when it comes to analyzing big South Texas whitetails, the length of the G-2 is critical. When that second tine off the main beam is equal in length or longer than the G-3 on a large-racked buck, I can be certain that the rack will score well. The buck before me, as best I could tell, definitely had a tall G-2 on his right side. But his left G-2 seemed short. If there were any other deductions from the deer's Boone and Crockett score, its chances of reaching that magical score of 170 would all but vanish.

For the first time, I began to question whether this was the deer I'd been waiting for all my life. It seems ludicrous to consider passing up such a buck, but my goal was a B&C trophy and, because of the exceptionally good conditions in South Texas, this year offered one of the best chances ever to get one. Now, I wasn't sure if this deer was the answer.

Suddenly, my deliberations were interrupted. Out of the corner of my eye, I spotted a large black feral hog striding across the disked strip behind the buck. I held my breath. These feral animals (domestic hogs gone wild) are common in the brush country, and they make deer skittish. In a flash, the buck jumped forward and darted to a sendero 30 yards away. Silhouetted against the Texas sky, he paused and looked back over his shoulder. There was no more time for debate. In another moment, the giant 12-pointer would disappear again. My instincts took over. The report from my 7mm Mag. shattered the quiet evening, and the buck of my dreams dropped to the ground.

As I approached the fallen buck, I felt real excitement but also the same bit of remorse I feel for each animal taken. He was a remarkable trophy, but I could see that his left G-2 was indeed a bit short. Well, even if he didn't make the book, he was a great buck.

After loading my deer and heading back to camp, I was greeted by David Morris, one of my long-time hunting companions. He looked at my deer and, without hesitation, said "Congratulations, Bob. I believe he is going to make it!"

With David's evaluation, my excitement continued to grow. During an impromptu measuring session, however, my buck fell short of a record-book score by a mere 1/8 of an inch. Though disappointed, I knew how lucky I was to actually see, let alone take, a buck like this.

The length of the G-2, or second tine, is the key factor in evaluating the size of a high-scoring whitetail in South Texas. If a buck has record-book proportions in terms of beam length, inside spread and tall tines, the G-2s will "make or break" the score. If the G-3s are tall and the G-2s extend upward just as far, you've found a high-scoring trophy buck.

But the deer's story didn't end there. Several busy weeks later, another wildlife intern, Rodney Glaze, took my buck to the Los Cazadores deer contest in Cotulla. I was more than a little surprised when Rodney called to tell me that my deer was not only leading the contest, but that its score had broken the 170 barrier, totalling 171 4/8 net. My emotions were back on the roller coaster.

Once the mandatory 60-day drying period had passed, official Boone and Crockett scorer John Stein measured the deer. The beautifully balanced rack scored 171 3/8, fulfilling my dream of a record-book buck. It wound up finishing first in the Los Cazadores net score division and was also recognized as the second-largest typical taken in Dimmit County in 1993. Overall, it was the third-best deer entered in Texas that year, according to the Texas Big Game Awards Program.

As a biologist and a hunter, I know that deer of this calibre are a rare and special breed. To actually take one is a privilege and one of the highlights of my life. I may never have another opportunity, but that's all right. I can savor this one forever.

CHAPTER THIRTEEN

Beating The Jinx

by Les Davenport

HALFWAY ACROSS THE FRIGID RIVER, as a torrent of numbingly cold water poured down my legs from a rip in my new chestwaders, it occurred to me that perhaps this just wasn't my day. After all, I'd already missed an open shot at a mammoth record-book whitetail, had two run-ins with trespassers who ruined my hunting plans and now I was soaked to the bone on a bitter December afternoon. What else could possibly go wrong?

I should have known better than to ask that question.

Maybe I was due for some bad luck, but I hadn't expected it all to come in one day. The previous year, in 1993, I'd taken four good bucks — two by bow and two by muzzleloader — that averaged 154 gross inches apiece. Some friends and I had been leasing two 350-acre tracts near my home in Woodford County, Illinois, and 1994 promised to be a great season. Life was good.

Indeed, that has been the case for many hunters in Illinois. Almost 100,000 deer are harvested each year in the Land of Lincoln, including a remarkable number of record-class trophies. Many deer experts believe this state has one of the healthiest and best-balanced herds in America. Good management by the state has helped make Illinois a mecca for trophy hunters.

That certainly wasn't the case when I was a boy. I can still remember the day in the late 1950s when my brother, Louis, and I spotted our

The author has taken many Illinois whitetails bigger than this 9-pointer, but none were any more rewarding or required harder hunting. After a season of mishaps, it represented a well-earned trophy. Photo courtesy of Les Davenport.

first deer track. Because whitetail sightings were almost unheard of at that time in central Illinois, we felt like celebrities. We were hooked.

When I was 15, I killed my first deer, an 8-pointer, on a gun hunt with my Dad in southern Illinois. By 1965, the year I graduated from high school, hunters took almost 8,000 deer in the state. I began bowhunting about that time and continued to progress as a hunter, and by the mid-1980s, I was badly smitten with trophy fever.

At the same time, Illinois' deer numbers were skyrocketing. When my son, Monte, was old enough, he also became addicted. At just 13 years of age, he shot his first deer, a beautiful 10-pointer scoring 143. After that, he took 20 more deer, 17 of them by bow, before moving on to West Point Military Academy and the 82nd Airborne. I sorely miss my long-time hunting partner. We shared some great hunting experiences.

In the Midwest, the "edges" where woodland meets prairie and/or crop field offer ideal habitat for whitetails. Add a nearby stream or lake, and you have perfect whitetail country. Be careful, however, not to push too deeply into the forest until the rut is in full swing. If you do, you'll push mature bucks out of their preferred haunts or force them to become totally nocturnal. Instead, hunt timbered points, corners or field edges prior to rutting activity.

But even without Monte, I had no reason to expect anything less than another rewarding season when '94 rolled around. Not only did I have two leases to hunt, but my wife, Connie, and I had also purchased a wooded farm in western Illinois. Each of the three farms had plenty of the type of edges between cropland, fields and woods that whitetails really like. I was ready.

But from the very start, fate seemed to be toying with me. During bow season, I spotted several big bucks, but for one reason or another, they all eluded me. Eventually, though, I found a deer that made me forget about all the others.

I'd seen his sign before. The big buck's rub line led from a thick bedding area, up an oak ridge and finally into a picked corn field where does congregated at twilight. With the prevailing wind in his face, the buck had a perfect setting for late-afternoon feeding forays to the food plot.

Given the choice between an above-average stand location with poor entry and exit lanes, or an average stand location with better-than-average approaches, choose the latter. If you disrupt deer to reach your stand or leave too much scent on your way in, you'll hurt your chances.

Just a few yards before the ridge sloped away into the corn field, I found what looked like a good place for an ambush. At a narrow spot in the trail, several white oaks provided perfect spots for a portable tree stand. Not only could I enter and exit the site quietly, but while in the stand, I figured my scent would waft over the ridge and avoid the buck's nose.

On the second afternoon, I saw him. He was a beautifully symmetrical 5x5! I waited motionlessly as he methodically picked his way through the underbrush, never veering from the trail that would lead him within 10 yards of my stand. I tried to breathe deeply as I felt my chest begin to tighten. He kept coming closer.

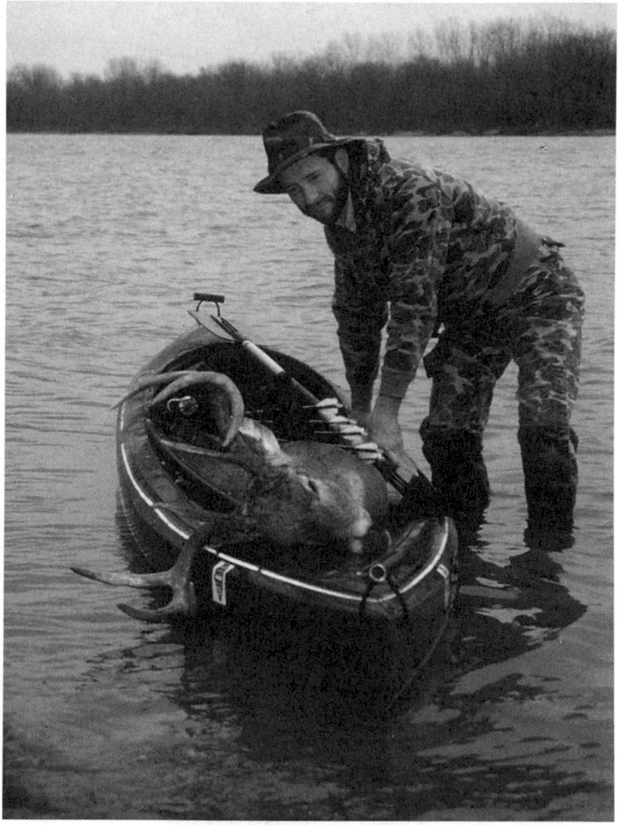

Being able to make a quiet approach to your hunting area is critical. The author often uses a kayak to enter and exit some of his favorite riverside hunting areas. Photo courtesy of Les Davenport.

At 15 paces, the big 10-pointer turned broadside and peered through the brush toward the harvested corn. He seemed to be searching for does. I had two choices: reposition myself and take the shot now or wait until he came a few steps closer and offered me a point-blank, quartering-away target. He didn't seem jumpy or suspicious, so I opted to wait for the quartering shot.

He turned his head back toward me and took a couple of steps closer to my stand. Just a few more feet, I thought, as my fingers tightened their grip on the bow. But suddenly, he made an unexpected 90-degree turn and began a shortcut toward the corn, still looking for does. A shot was impossible. Moments later, he walked away and was gone. The perfect 10, my "Bo Derek" buck, never reappeared. Luck, I was reminded, is like the morning dew on a pasture - some settles on the flowers and some on cow manure. I was beginning to feel seriously jinxed.

Illinois' first three-day firearms season falls during the rut in November and equally divides the 14-week archery season. About a decade earlier, I had given up hunting during this shotgun season because there just seemed to be too many orange jackets and too much friendly fire in the small woodlots of Woodford County. But when my buddies and I began

Working "the edges" is a key to taking pre-rut bucks like this one claimed by the author. If your hunting efforts penetrate too far into the woods before the rut, you may spook mature bucks out of the area. Stick to the fringes until then. Photo courtesy of Les Davenport.

leasing some ground in 1992, the firearm season seemed a safer proposition. I started muzzleloading that year, looking for the same kind of one-shot challenge I enjoyed with bowhunting.

This gun season would be special because Connie, my wife, would be joining me for the first time. As recently as August, she had never even fired a gun. But by opening day, my petite 100-pound spouse could dot an "i" at 40 yards with a .50-caliber muzzleloader. She decided to restrict her shots to that range and proclaimed herself ready to hunt.

Opening morning found us sitting side by side in a permanent tree blind on our farm. It was a bluebird day, and unbelievably, there was no gun pressure on any of the adjacent land. Does, birds and squirrels entertained us, but no bucks showed up. Connie enjoyed daybreak in the woods, and she began, I think, to understand my passion for deer hunting.

We hunted separately that afternoon, with Connie in a ground blind near an old oil rig. Just before sunset, a keeper 8-pointer meandered into a picked bean field and laid down 50 yards from her blind. He watched does mill around until a bigger buck appeared and confronted him. The competing males locked antlers and sparred just inside the timber until after dark.

"Why didn't you shoot?" I asked later.

"I thought about it," Connie replied, "but the distance looked a little too far. Anyway, it was fun watching them."

She went home empty-handed that day, but what great restraint for a novice hunter! She wanted to be successful but not at the price of wounding a deer.

I spied two "shooter" bucks in the next two days, but both were out of range. The jinx seemed to be perpetuating itself, at least in my mind. The final four-day gun season would open in two weeks. Would we be shut out again?

When it comes to taking a shot at a deer, don't let excitement overcome your common sense. Resist the temptation to "talk yourself into" attempting a shot that has a low probability of success. Wounding deer with low-percentage shots is just not acceptable. Success, ethics and peace of mind are all by-products of patience.

Thursday, December 1 dawned cold and windy, with no clues as to what a strange day it would become. Connie had to work so I would be hunting on my own that day. I decided to spend the morning in a portable tree stand that was ideally situated on one of the Woodford leases. Bucks tended to filter past the location when entering and exiting a bedding area, and a 150-inch deer had eluded me at that spot earlier in the bow season. In '93, a 9-pointer tempted fate there. He now hangs on my wall.

It was barely daylight when, positioned in my stand, I heard crunching noises coming from my right. Deer fled the bedding area from every direction. Within minutes, a trespassing hunter appeared from the thicket. The man rattled off a list of excuses. I, in turn, reminded him that this was his second blatant crossing of the property line and that no further clemency would be granted him if there were a third offense.

The damage already had been done. The trampled bedding area made it unlikely that a mature buck would now show up, and the other two leaseholders were already stationed in the only other timbered areas where I could relocate on that tract. After two uneventful hours, I decided to abandon the site and hunt the second lease a few miles away. It would be a better afternoon site anyway, and there were no other leaseholders there that day.

My game plan was set. I would still-hunt three particular thickets during the late morning then finish the day in a tree stand I had recently set up across the river. But, I had barely started to still-hunt when yet another wayward hunter appeared! When questioned, he announced that the owner had granted him permission to hunt there — seven years ago! Had he bothered to reconfirm, the owner would have told him that the land was now under lease. The man left but not until he had tromped through the entire west end of the lease.

Resignation began to set in. Would anything go right today?

Three hours of still-hunting turned up 18 does but nothing with horns. The best buck haunt, however, was still ahead in a willow slough at the river's edge. A fellow leaseholder, who was not prone to exaggeration, had told me he'd twice seen a "giant" buck on its outskirts.

Fortunately, a strong southwest wind made the slough approachable. Step by step, I slowly eased my way through the waist-high fescue that surrounded the slough. My eyes kept scanning for any part of an antler, ear or leg. When two deer erupted from the cover nearby, my heart skipped a beat before I realized they were yearlings. They bounded along a river dike and disappeared into a stand of horse weeds.

Suddenly, out of the thick grass about 60 yards ahead, a giant ivory hatrack appeared. It was a monster non-typical! He was just inside the willow thicket, watching the two yearlings that had just fled. I could tell from his body language that he had no idea of my presence. Hammer back, I centered the sights of my muzzleloader on the buck's

When still-hunting, train yourself to look for portions of a deer's extremities, such as a flicking ear, a white throat patch, antler tips or a black nose. It's especially important to study an area from more than one vantage point. This often requires a second pass-through from a different angle. Highly pressured bucks may not budge until your eyes meet theirs.

chest. As the gun fired, the buck spun 180 degrees and charged straight for me like a runaway locomotive!

If you've ever witnessed a muzzleloader being reloaded by a man with 10 thumbs, it's not a pretty picture. As I desperately tried to prepare for another shot, the buck kept coming, finally veering off just a few feet before he reached me. He finally stopped in an open field 50 yards to my left. Meanwhile, I had powder poured on the barrel, down the gun and on the ground, with a .50-caliber ball in one hand and the ram rod halfway out of its saddle.

Apparently unscathed and unconcerned, the giant buck trotted back to the willow slough and disappeared. That had to be the biggest buck in the county. How had I missed? What went wrong? Why me? I felt like the spurned victim in a country-western song.

I found an explanation when I examined the area where the buck had been standing. My shot had hit the trunk of a willow tree about six inches to the left of the deer. The echo of the gunshot must have reverberated off the dike and fooled the buck into retreating in the wrong direction. I desperately wanted to replay the last 10 minutes of my life, but that would be like trying to unring a bell.

Even now, that miss still haunts me. Here was a deer with a 25-inch inside spread, a heavy 5x5 frame and sticker and kicker points jutting out everywhere. A sure 200-inch-plus Boone & Crockett trophy, one of the most massive racks I've seen in 32 years of hunting.

Afterwards, while drinking a soda at the truck, I tried to compose myself and figure out what to do. After what had transpired so far, I wasn't sure if I should continue to hunt the rest of the day. At this point, it seemed as pointless as polishing the decks of the Titanic. Apparently, this jinx was stronger than I had imagined. After all, it had deflected a .50-caliber lead ball right into a willow tree. Then, I remembered one of my favorite phrases: "Opportunity doesn't sail in on a ship. It comes from within. Opportunity rarely looks like an opportunity. Often, it is disguised as misfortune, defeat and rejection." I decided to head into the field again.

To get to the tree stand I wanted to hunt for the final hours of the day, I had to ford the river. By the time I realized that there was a half-inch rip in the crotch of my new $120 chestwaders, ice-cold river water had encircled my legs. It felt as if a cold hand had reached inside of me and grabbed my stomach.

Shivering as I slogged up the opposite bank, I considered my options. It was too late to return home and change, and the day was winding down. So, naked from the waist down on a December afternoon, I stood on the riverbank and wrung out two layers of clothes. At that moment, I would have gladly paid $50, maybe $75, for dry longjohns and socks.

After getting dressed and taking a few deep breaths, I was back on my way and soon in my tree stand. At least now, I thought, I could stay put for the rest of the day. But after only a few seconds in my stand, I spotted another hunter just 100 yards east of me, hunting an adjoining property. Not good! He was undoubtedly hoping to shoot a deer coming from my direction toward a clover field. Meanwhile, I was hoping to drop a mature buck before it crossed the property line into the same field. If he pulled the trigger on a deer I let pass, the day's hunt would pretty much be over. If I didn't shoot, he probably would.

Some stands and even tracts are better for morning hunting, while others may be good afternoon sites. The predominant wind direction and the position of a bedding or staging area will influence your choice. But, a good hunter always tries to have several stand locations available and picks the best one for the situation each day. Overuse of one site can spook deer, too. By using several different locations, a hunter becomes less predictable and prevents stand burn-out.

I would have worried about this "Catch-22" even more, but I was becoming preoccupied with the fact that the frigid wind was gradually numbing by damp legs and feet. The other hunter must have been cold, too. He kept moving about his stand, rubbing his shoulders and trying to stay warm.

The minutes crawled past until finally, with only about 30 minutes before legal quitting time, a nice buck suddenly materialized in front of me. But, he was on the wrong side of the fence. It certainly wouldn't be right to shoot across the boundary and trespass to claim the animal, so the buck was off-limits. I had no choice but to bite the bullet, so to speak.

This buck could have taught flirtation to Madonna. The beautiful 5x4 browsed casually just 30 yards in front me and I could do nothing. So far, a brushy knoll had prevented the other hunter from seeing the deer, but at any moment, the deer would crest the knoll and be in clear view of the other hunter. At least then, I figured, I could go home and take a hot

The author, who lives and hunts in central Illinois, poses with eight of his best bow-killed bucks. He believes persistence, more than any other trait, defines the successful trophy hunter. Photo courtesy of Les Davenport.

shower. I was beginning to shake uncontrollably from the cold.

The buck topped the knoll and began picking his way through the shoulder-high brush. I looked toward the hunter, expecting to hear a shot, but just as the deer came into his view, he began climbing down from his tree stand! With 15 minutes of shooting time remaining, the cold must have finally gotten to him. He never saw the buck.

The deer saw him, however. It dropped into a sneaking posture, then bounded toward me and jumped the fence onto the lease. He stopped momentarily to look about. That was all I needed. Even with the quakes, it was a no-brainer shot. The buck lunged once and dropped. Could I be dreaming? The jinx had finally been beaten.

The 5x4 wound up with a gross score of 141 1/8 inches, but I couldn't have been any happier if he'd measured 241 inches. After everything I'd gone through to take that deer, I was pretty proud of him.

Connie and I both ate tags at season's end but not before passing up another "iffy" shot at a dandy 10-pointer. The season wasn't everything we'd hoped for, but it was still special for both of us. And, we knew that we'd try it all again next season. With or without the jinx!